FOSTERING THE HEART

NIKI BARLOW

Hearts Above Home Press

Dedication

I dedicate this book to my foster children; you changed my life. I will always love you. To my husband who walked this path daily with me I thank you for your leadership and strength. To my children, extended family, and friends who gave us encouragement, support, and prayers when we decided to take in our beautiful foster children. I recognize our decision changed your lives too, yet you jumped in and loved our new family. Thank you to the case workers, counselors, and advocates who devote their lives to make positive change in the futures of children.

This sixty-day devotional is a journey through the daily life of foster care. With 31 years as a parent and eight years of foster parenting, I use my experiences of trial and error to help you through unique situations. I love children and believe they are capable of amazing things. I pray these devotionals will encourage, uplift, and stir your mind to becoming the best Foster Parent you can be.

Table of Contents

Introduction

"Children are a heritage from the LORD, offspring a reward from him."

-Psalm 127:3

Night cloaked the neighborhood in a dull-gray haze. The dust lining the cement drive swirled about her scuffed and tattered shoes. The child stepped closer to the door, pulling her life in an oversized, blue plastic bag. The building loomed larger with each heartbeat.

She wanted to go home. At least there, she knew what to expect. Her bedroom closet with the hidden nest of blankets; Mr. Snuggles, matted from years' worth of tears; and a few scattered goldfish snacks. What would this new house bring?

If it were like the last placements, she and her siblings would leave this place too. The first called her temporary, whatever that meant. The second was mad when she made them sick. She didn't care. The couch was hard, and the loud talking kept her awake at night. The last home, she heard them whispering how hard it was taking care of them. It was not what they expected. Oh, they wanted to keep sissy, but not all of them. Approaching the door, she bit her lip, would they realize the truth. She had to be bad cause no one wanted her.

The thoughts of children entering foster care vary, but the uncertainty of the future is a common thread. Foster parents are in the trenches, the first line of defense to change the odds of these children's lives. Statistics show an increase of homelessness, teen pregnancy, abuse, drug/alcohol use (Stout, 2012), prison time, dropout rates, or sex trafficking for foster kids. These rates increase with children who age out of the foster care system without adoption or returning to their families (Brown, 2024).

There is no one theory or a single hug which will change a child's life. But together, we can face the daily challenges of foster parenting. Our compassionate love fills us with the desire to help a child. We prepare ourselves with knowledge and prayer. The days can get hard as our resilience diminishes in the fight. Isaiah 40:29 tells us, "He gives strength to the weary and increases the power of the weak." Only God has the answer to heal a child's heart.

This devotional is meant to encourage. It is a representation of taking one day and each moment at a time. Honesty with trial-and-error experience fills the pages with small steps provided towards resolving ongoing issues of foster children.

My prayer for you, as you love these at-risk children, is for you to go beyond providing tangible security. May God, help you fight the battles the kids cannot, provide them with hope, and lead them towards healing. The Lord will lift you up with His might, wisdom, and courage to sustain you. He will give you the blessing of seeing your hard work and love transform the lives of these beautiful kids.

Navigating to
a New Beginning

1
Are We Doing Enough?

*"'Call to me and I will answer you and tell you great and
unsearchable things you do not know.'"*

-Jeremiah 33:3

The morning sun peaked over the horizon as my husband, and
I joined hands in prayer. Nothing unusual, we did it every day. It was
the prayer laid on our hearts which startled me: "God, are we doing
enough?" It was a crazy idea—we were too busy already.

Our lives revolved around ministry. My husband, a community
pastor, worked overtime counseling, visiting hospitals and jails, leading
home churches, cooking hundreds of church dinners, and directing
outreach projects. I led a Christian writers' group, hoped to publish a
book, helped with church functions, took care of our home, and ran a
small fulltime business.

Since our kids were in college, we used the extra bedrooms in
our home to house young adults who came to our community to work
during the tourist season. When we first started questioning whether
we should do more, our natural reaction was to provide lodging for
more summer residents. Although it was not apparent how we could
stick one more thing into the mix, God knew better than we did. We
trusted He would get us through.

Years ago, we'd considered having an additional child, or
adopting. We decided against it because as a blended family of four
children, dog, and cat, our lives were full.

When God answered our prayer, He took the accumulation of
our lifetime and an old dream and brought it all full circle, building it

into this one moment. He searched our hearts, minds, and our faith to fulfill His purpose.

Three weeks after that sunrise prayer time together, our lives changed forever. God gave us the gift of three foster children. Reflecting now, I see how God had prepared us over the years in unique ways for this one crucial moment. He continues to use this life to refine us and draw us deeper into our relationship with Him. He showed us a world most people miss, and I am thankful.

This was not the answer to my prayers that I expected or wanted, but God chose my husband and I to teach us great and unsearchable things. Over the next few years, He would develop us to love beyond ourselves, give us unforeseen wisdom, and bind us close together.

I encourage you to talk to God. Ask Him to show you the secrets of your heart. Be open to His answer and follow Him. Do not fear; God will give you all the tools you need to accomplish His calling. He is a great teacher. Without God we would not have been able to offer the love the children needed. He provided all knowledge, strength, courage, patience, and kindness we needed, and He will for you as well. He knows your past, your today, and your tomorrow. God will walk beside you and show you everything you need.

> *Dear Abba Papa, You know us better than we know ourselves. You see the secret desires of our hearts. We ask this day for You to reveal to us our callings. Remove our fear so we may have peace as we step into our future. May we always walk hand in hand with You. Help us to stay firm, even when You ask us to do something, we think is impossible. Thank You, God, for the work we will do together. Amen.*

Fostering the Heart Action

Openly pray for what is in your heart. If you have a desire which is in line with God's word, start to pursue it, but be open to God changing your plans to fit His. If you do not take a step forward, you will never move and a year from now nothing will have changed. Take fifteen minutes today to prepare for what you believe God is calling you to. Schedule time for the next day to intentionally move forward. Continue this pattern and see what God does with your life.

Going Deeper in Scripture: 1 Corinthians 2:10-11; Romans 11:33-34; Deuteronomy 29:29

Your Thoughts

_____

_____

_____

_____

_____

_____

_____

_____

_____

_____

_____

_____

_____

_____

_____

_____

2
The Whisper

"The Lord came and stood there, calling as at the other times,
"Samuel! Samuel!" Then Samuel said, "Speak, for your servant
is listening." And the Lord said to Samuel: "See, I am about to
do something in Israel that will make the ears of everyone who
hears about it tingle."

-1 Samuel 3:10-11

Growing up, I had a cool rope swing. It soared over a lush, green gully. On my nineteenth birthday, I stood on the back porch with a friend. He asked me to go on the rope swing. A voice whispered in my head; don't go.

I wrestled with my thoughts. Why not? I've done this so many times.

My friend tugged on my hand. Giving in to the pressure, I told myself I was being ridiculous.

I climbed on. With a push, the swing flew out over the ravine. The rope snapped.

Landing at an odd angle, I hit the ground. Jarring pain shot up my spine. I was unable to move.

Ignoring God's leadership led to profound consequences. I had crushed five vertebrae.

Sometimes when God speaks to me, He must shout in my ear, jumping up and down, waving His arms to get my attention. Just like Samuel, I need to hear His voice three times, so I can get it through my head and hear Him clearly.

He may use major events; like accidents, illness, divorce, or unemployment to get us to listen. But often, God whispers or gives a little nudge to prepare us for a future event in our lives.

During morning devotions with my husband, I heard God.

He whispered, "Be prepared. Trials are coming."

As empty nesters with adult children, my first thought was something would happen to one of them. *What God? No, not again. Please, nothing terrible.*

He nudged me with reassurance, "it won't necessarily be bad, just hard."

I took a breath, Ok God, I can handle that if You want me to.

This was God preparing me for the next obedience call He gave me. It was kind of Him to give me a warning, to allow me to prepare. I'll admit I worried a bit about the unknown event to take place, and I prayed for God to keep my children safe. But I believed He would guide me, and soon He revealed the secret: three foster children.

When God speaks, we choose whether to listen or not. It's easy when it fits into our schedule, but when He tells us we are taking in trauma children, which is in high contrast to our peaceful life, we may want to refuse.

With the swing incident, I reasoned my way out of acting as God called. The consequences taught me to listen intently to His words. When He whispered a warning, I knew to take it seriously. Open to His will, I waited and trusted He would sustain us through the hardships.

At other times, His voice is a stormy stirring of uncomfortable feeling you can't quite make out. When His leadership feels like this, stop, quiet your mind from outside distraction, and wait until you hear with your heart.

God speaks to us through prayer, family and friends, circumstances, and even through strangers. When we study the Bible, God gives us the ability to differentiate between our emotions, the world's pulling, and His leading, so stay close to His Word and listen. He wants to lead you. Let Him.

> *Father, may we open our ears to hear this day. Give us wisdom, direction, and the assurance You are near. We ask You, Lord, to prepare our hearts and minds for Your next calling and wisdom to discern the difference between Your whisper and the enemy's misguidance. We praise You and thank you for preparing us to do Your will. Amen.*

Fostering the Heart Action

Find an area in the house or outside where you can sit in quiet, and you will not be interrupted. Start with a prayer asking God to open your ears to hear and your heart to accept what He wants to tell you. Write down your thoughts. Over the next couple of days, let it resonate with you. Repeat this exercise until you clearly hear from the Lord.

Going Deeper in Scripture: Isaiah 29:23; Proverbs 2:1-5; James 1:22

Your Thoughts

_____
_____
_____
_____
_____
_____
_____
_____
_____
_____

3
Answering the Call

"For we are God's handiwork, created in Christ Jesus to do good works, which God prepared in advance for us to do."
-Ephesians 2:10

My husband picked up the phone. "Rocky Mountain Church, can I help you?" Over the next few moments, the human services representative explained their need. They were looking for someone to take in three foster kids, and they asked to place the information in the church bulletin. After explaining that he needed more details before fulfilling the request, they decided my husband would attend a meeting the next day.

I was across the globe basking in the sun on a Mediterranean cruise with my parents and unreachable by phone when I received the email: "We need to talk."

My heart stopped for a minute before the thought hit me: logically, if anything happened to our family, he would call the ship. Reassured, I sent back a message, "Can you give me a little more information?" A few hours later the reply came, "I believe God is calling us to take in three young foster children. They were removed from their family and need a home by next weekend."

Alrighty then. Nothing like a little decision to make which will affect every portion of my life. Knowing my husband is led by the Holy Spirit, the answer was simple, "If you believe it's God's will, I trust you. Of course, we can take them."

The details were unimportant. I trusted God. Later I would wonder what I was thinking, but at the time it felt God-breathed. He created us to do His good works here on Earth, crafting our lives in preparation for the journey. We are a lump of clay molded into a living sculpture—caressed, nurtured, and sometimes pummeled into God's creation.

God knows our past, present, and future. He prepared a plan before we were ever born. Knowing us so intimately, He can fulfill our own and others' needs better than we can. He placed these children with us because of our unique circumstances. It was an accumulation of our prior life events, knowledge of the Bible, and compassion which brought these specific children to us.

God calls all of us to care for orphans, but many people turn away. Be prepared, for you have been chosen by God to answer with *yes* when He calls you to a child's life. He will not leave you alone but will walk with you through your obedience to Him. He will guide you every second as you parent the hurting children of the world. If each of us listened to God's desires, there would be no unloved children. There is nothing better in this world than to take part in His plan. When it appears overwhelming, lean into God, and trust the Lord of the universe to pull the pieces of the children's lives and your life together for a greater purpose.

> *God, we do not understand the ways of the world. And we may not be able to see how You can use all things for Your good works. But we come to you with confidence that You want to form us into your image. Protect us from the enemy who would like us to leave Your path. Give us wisdom, love, and strength to walk in the ways You have prepared for us. Amen.*

Fostering the Heart Action

Look back over your life. When were the moments God did something unexpected? Today, focus on seeing God when He does little things throughout the day. Before you go to bed, reflect on these with a spouse or friend. How could God use these moments to fulfil part of His plan?

Going Deeper in Scripture: Matthew 22:14; John 15:16; Romans 8:28

Your Thoughts

_____

_____

_____

_____

_____

_____

_____

_____

_____

_____

_____

_____

_____

_____

_____

_____

_____

_____

_____

_____

_____

_____

_____

4

Step into God's Plan

"For I know the plans I have for you," declares the Lord, "plans to prosper you and not to harm you, plans to give you hope and a future."

-Jeremiah 29:11

Placing a hand on my midsection, I tried to still the riptide of emotion. So many feelings battled within me. Excitement for the new adventures and the promise of hope as we stepped by faith into parenting foster children collided with the nausea of fearing all the unknown that lay ahead.

In a whirlwind, my husband and I had done the legwork, cleaned the rooms, added new beds and bedding, purchased a used dresser, and stocked the pantry. Now, we nervously waited at the window for the arrival of our new foster children. Pacing, I reminded myself it was only for six months. We could love little children, give them a home, and walk with their parents while they take the necessary measures to become healthy.

Whenever we move out of our comfort zones, we are challenged and will grow exponentially. Fear of the unknown can hold us back. Ephesians 5 tells us a plan for moving forward. We are to be careful how we live, be wise, make the most of our opportunities, and pray for understanding of the Lord's will.

With anticipation, foster parents prepare for foster children by taking classes, seeking wise council, predicting what the child will need physically and emotionally, and getting our house ready, but the one thing we cannot produce on our own is God's plan. Proverbs 16:9

states, "In their hearts humans plan their course, but the LORD establishes their steps." He intervenes to bring the specific child to us at an exact time. Each child comes from different circumstances, and God chooses us to care for that child for a reason. We can try to predict what will take place, but in the end, we simply need to go with the ebb and flow of the children and the situation.

All our planning cannot take away the nerves which come with unexpected circumstances. We can trust God to be there for us with strength, wisdom, and faithfulness through all the trials and blessings of raising foster children. Romans 8:31 asks, "What, then, shall we say in response to these things? If God is for us, who can be against us?" With God on our side, we can step out with assurance to complete the task before us and love these kids the way they need to be loved.

We all have a certain amount of time to live. We can choose to make a positive difference for others, or we can let the days slide by, never knowing what we were capable of accomplishing. Becoming a foster parent is a risk. You open your heart, home, time, security, and life. Being obedient to God to raise a foster child will never go unrewarded. Over time, you will become stronger, patient, and kinder.

God has a plan for you. He uses all things in our lives, whether good or bad, to increase our reliance on Him, our faith in Him, and to produce a desire within us to lead others to Him, because we know how much better life is when we follow Jesus. He offers us hope and a future.

Father God, we come to You expecting to be used to achieve the purpose of raising a foster child for Your glory. We recognize that our plans may conflict with Your wants, so give us strength and willingness to put aside our selfish desires and follow You. Help us to be the best foster parents we can be and to go beyond our limited viewpoint to accomplish Your goals. Amen.

Fostering the Heart Action

Spend fifteen minutes praying. Be open-minded. Ask God to reveal His plan and for guidance in how to implement it. If you are unsure, educate yourself on the area you feel is lacking or talk to someone associated with foster care for advice.

Going Deeper in Scripture: Ephesians 5:15-17; James 4:14; 1 Thessalonians 2:11-12

Your Thoughts

_____

_____

_____

_____

_____

_____

_____

_____

_____

_____

_____

_____

_____

_____

_____

_____

_____

_____

5
Build a Team

"Two are better than one,
because they have a good return for their labor:
If either of them falls down,
one can help the other up.
But pity anyone who falls
and has no one to help them up.
Though one may be overpowered,
two can defend themselves.
A cord of three strands is not quickly broken."
-Ecclesiastes 4:9-10, 12

My husband is a pastor, so frankly, we stumbled into building a cord of three strands. The people of our church were wonderful. They rallied around our decision to foster, providing us prayer, laundry soap, food, clothes, and encouragement. While social services work to give foster parents the necessary tools to be a success, they cannot fill every need. We, the body of Christ, need to join to serve foster children.

Soon after we began fostering, a beautiful lady approached me at church. She said, "I really think what you're doing is wonderful. I could never do it. I'm not good with children, but I am a good shopper. Can we bring you some groceries?"

My initial reaction was, *we have this under control; we don't need help.* But the earnestness on her face sent a different message; God was calling me to allow her to serve in the capacity in which He had gifted her. As the months began to roll by, her help became vital. Shopping is time-consuming and expensive. With foster care meetings, counseling, working, and daily life with three additional, traumatized kids, the days were short, and money was stretched.

There will be times when you wonder how you will make it through. When the screaming, anger, lies, and focusing issues become overwhelming. This is when you will need your team. When you have a cord of three or more, you are blessed to have people with various abilities.

There are friends with whom we can honestly vent, knowing they will not judge, and the conversation will stay private. Others are prayer warriors ready to hit their knees at a moment's notice. Encouragers send cards or stop us in passing with the right words to lift our spirits, at the exact time we need it. You may ask someone to be on your team, who you later discover has misconceptions about foster children. Rather than being angry, use these moments to teach and address falsehoods, but realize these may not be the people to help.

God gave us distinct roles. "Each of you should use whatever gift you have received to serve others, as faithful stewards of God's grace in its various forms" (1 Peter 4:10).

Look for people who have unique abilities to walk alongside you. Are there babysitters for a night off, tutors to mentor the child, current foster parents who can advise you, or people with servant hearts? You are not meant to fill every needed role. God gave you a special calling only few can do. Make sure you are not one of the statistics of failure, but a life-giver to the child who will come into your home.

My husband and I can lift each other up out of the pit, but we need the complete cord of three to get through the rough times of raising traumatized kids. Seek out people to help, matching their talents with the right needs.

> *Lord, we pray for the people who will come alongside us to raise Your child. Help us to accept help, realizing this is not a reflection of our inability, but an image of Your love and provision. We ask You to unite us by preparing our hearts and minds. We recognize foster children need multiple loving*

individuals in their lives. Thank You in advance for the relationships we will form. Amen.

Fostering the Heart Action

Start now to form your team. Make a list of people who can support you in a variety of ways. Not sure who those people are? Let friends, family, a local church, and neighbors know what you plan to do. Invite them to pray for you. Ask them if they might be able to come alongside the children. Be transparent! God will use your honesty to testify to the people surrounding you.

Going Deeper in Scripture: 3 John 1:8; Hebrews 10:24; Ephesians 4:16

Your Thoughts

_____

_____

_____

_____

_____

_____

_____

_____

_____

_____

_____

6
Arrival Day

"Religion that God our Father accepts as pure and faultless is
this: to look after orphans and widows in their distress and to
keep oneself from being polluted by the world."

-James 1:27

Our foster children came to us after previous homes. They
were first placed with a family friend, but when it became apparent the
stay would be long, they were moved. The second couple's good
intentions were complicated by a small apartment, a new city, and a
large daycare center. To top it off, everyone got the flu. The children
felt lost.

After two weeks, the search for another place began. Human
services had the option of a group house, but felt it was not a good
placement for these siblings. They were desperate to keep them
together, so with options dwindling, they reached out to several
churches. The kids expected to go home to their parents, but God had
different plans for them.

When we heard of their plight, compassion led us to offer to
take them. On arrival day, a seven-, six-, and three-year-old walked into
our home, accompanied by their case worker, holding big blue
disposable bags. The ragged remains of their previous life. My heart
cried out for these little ones.

After the close quarters of their previous placement, the eldest
child was excited to get their own room. The two littles shared a
bedroom with two new twin beds covered with purple heart

comforters. Used to sharing a single bed, they loved having their own space.

The truth below the surface emotions was different, however. They were apprehensive, scared, and confused.

Not knowing what to expect from foster care, we invited the children's parent over to help settle them in. The parent helped unpack their belongings. We wanted the children to know we were not taking away their parent. This began a long relationship of learning and maturing with the parent.

The little ones still ill, we snuggled them into bed early. After saying prayers, we reminded them they were safe, and invited them to come get us if they needed anything. It would be months before they would feel comfortable enough to disturb our sleep at night for help.

In foster care, they stress our number one priority is safety. Beyond that, it is up to you to be the parent these children need. Loving them with consistency promotes security and teaches them to be able to predict reactions. These are gifts you can give them immediately.

Set a time schedule for eating, like three regular meals and two snacks. Some foster children come from homes where they fed themselves, even when young. They may feel insecure if they do not have access to food. They will realize they can count on you to provide this basic need.

Establish bath time routines to promote healthy habits. Do not assume they will understand why; explain it to them.

Be adamant about bedtimes. It gives you freedom to rest. When the kids know what to expect, they respond much better to every aspect of life.

It will take time to gain trust and break the patterns of the past that hold them captive. Reliability of schedules and repeated words of assurance teach them they can rely on you. Knowing they have food consistently, being allowed uninterrupted nights of sleep, and seeing you provide safety with locked windows and doors shows them what to expect. Teaching them of God's love lets them know they will never be alone.

God, grant us wisdom. Let us see beyond ourselves, into the world the children come from. We may never understand their past home life, but we can provide a stable future. Please provide us with tools to love these children with consistency, grace, and understanding beyond our worldly knowledge. Amen.

Fostering the Heart Action

Ask the case worker about the child. Try to greet them with personalized touches. For example, a football for a football player or a stuffed animal for a little one. If it is short notice, ask a friend to go to the store. Prepare by getting the immediate items the children need to survive. When they first walk into your house, take time to greet them, show them around, and make sure they know they are important.

Going Deeper in Scripture: Psalm 91:2; Psalm 4:8; Psalm 10:14

Your Thoughts

_____
_____
_____
_____
_____
_____
_____
_____
_____

7
Giving Generously

"Remember this: Whoever sows sparingly will also reap sparingly, and whoever sows generously will also reap generously."
-2 Corinthians 9:6

Whether you invest in one child or many, you are doing the will of God. The Bible tells us God accepts looking after orphans in their distress as pure and faultless. Each child saved represents not only that one child, but generations to follow. When we effectively change a foster child's life for the better, it sows seeds into all who meet them today and tomorrow.

As foster parents, we love, nurture, and bring our kids up to stand on their own feet in a healthy, life-giving manner. If we slide along the surface doing the minimum of safety, food, and shelter instead of going deep to help them heal, uplift their self-esteem, and nurture to combat trauma issues, we shortchange them and ourselves. God uses them to draw us deeper in faith, strength, patience, and generosity. Look into the face of your beautiful children, and know you are making a difference by helping them to learn trust, self-esteem, family, and faith.

On this day I am thankful God felt I was able to be a foster parent. But that is not always so. Sometimes I am tired. I would love the uncomplicated way instead of the challenge. If only I could have permission to act selfish, not caring, holding tight to what I want out of life. We were not made that way. God gave us compassion and an ability to discern right from wrong. When we give more than we think we are capable of, it is the ultimate act of loving God.

Growing up, I was taught that the things most worth having were the things you worked the hardest for. When you earned them, you appreciated them to the fullest. As parents, we need to show through our actions and instruct the kids not to take the easy path but the best. It is like ice skating you can skootch across the cold surface on your back end or stand and dig the ice skate blade into the frozen pond, then push off to gain speed. When the child falls, we give them a hand up, but then let them try repeatedly, until they can glide across the ice. Foster children may take what appears to be an easy way out: to hide their pain beneath alcohol or drugs, to express anger through hurting others, or to lie to avoid consequences.

Breaking past habits is not easy. We must go beyond keeping our kids safe, to teaching them to stand. God knows us intimately. He will show us how to set goals, follow a course, and achieve joy while doing it. Kindness goes a long way toward helping dysfunctional children learn to be functional. A happy smile even when things are not going our way teaches them it's okay to struggle. We are not defined by a moment, but how our character comes through when handling difficult circumstances.

As time goes on, God raises up new situations. Will you become overwhelmed with future situations, or will you take them and give generously? This is the difference between reaping sparingly and abundantly. Between following God's will and following your own. Digging deep within our souls to meet the challenge of foster parenting will change lives.

Lord, it is not within me to sacrifice my life for another. Help me to see through Your eyes. Give me Your power and might to fulfill Your perfect plan. Let me give generously, with an open heart. Thank You for allowing me to be a foster parent to a child worth believing in. Help me to show them Your great love and give them hope for the future.

Fostering the Heart Action

The next time you have a gut reaction to not do something because it appears too hard, stop. Pray, and give it a few days of thought before you commit one way or another. Ask God to give you, His perspective.

Going Deeper in Scripture: 1 Timothy 6:18; Matthew 10:42; James 1:27

Your Thoughts

_____

_____

_____

_____

_____

_____

_____

_____

_____

_____

_____

_____

_____

_____

8

A Sense of Home

"...till the Spirit is poured on us from on high,
and the desert becomes a fertile field,
and the fertile field seems like a forest.
The Lord's justice will dwell in the desert,
his righteousness live in the fertile field.
The fruit of that righteousness will be peace;
its effect will be quietness and confidence forever.
My people will live in peaceful dwelling places,
in secure homes,
in undisturbed places of rest."

-Isaiah 32:15-18

As a little girl, I would wake up snuggled under warm covers in a soft bed. The smell of coffee permeating the air and the sound of my mother moving about the kitchen gave me the assurance I was safe, loved, and home.

One night, I said prayers and tucked my foster child in bed. The child said, "I always know when to get up in the morning because I hear you making coffee." It made me smile to think my foster child knows safety, too, that they are loved, and that this is what home should feel like.

For many of these kids, their households were fear-based. They were afraid to face what was outside their bed covers. Would it be a good day, or bad? They may have to deal with yelling, turmoil trying to get ready for school, tiptoeing to get food without waking a grumpy parent, or hiding out in a cold neighborhood to avoid problems. They lived in a desert of dried-up emotions, prickly pain, and thirsting for water. In our homes, they should see a fertile forest where roots of peace, quietness, and confidence can grow, filling their souls.

We cannot get justice for the desert they came from, even though we may want to. We can pray for change in the hearts of their family, encourage them to get concrete help, and when necessary, provide facts to the proper authority. Only God will decide their fate. Justice may come here on Earth or eternally in heaven or hell. Foster parents must put aside their own sense of justice and focus on the love and healing of the children.

Some of us are morning people, and it is easy to get up with a smile as we prepare breakfast, find misplaced shoes, gather homework, or deal with a child who does not want to go to school. Others have a tough time facing a new morning without two cups of coffee, a shower, and complete quiet. Acknowledge which type of person you are and adjust your schedule to fit the needs of the kids. You are their first contact, which will set the tone for their entire day. If you are impatient, they will be. If you are angry, they will be. If you are agitated, they will be.

Plan to rise early. Extra time takes pressure off everyone. Prepare at night with clothes ready for the next day, lunches done, and homework in backpacks in a designated area. Turn on Christian music during breakfast or on the car ride to school. It helps start a rhythm of peace for the day. Be uplifting and encouraging. Routine cannot be over-emphasized. Kids who know what to expect in the morning will do better throughout the day.

> *Father, give us wisdom, perseverance, and gentleness to show our foster children what home truly is. Let them feel safe and open to express their innermost feelings, not what they think they should share because of their past. We pray we will receive their words well, teaching them they are important, listened to, and loved. Help us to provide a peaceful dwelling place, a secure home, where our foster children can have undisturbed rest, so they may heal, grow, and know what a home is. Amen.*

Fostering the Heart Action

Get up earlier than you normally do, take time to read the Bible, pray, and center yourself before you need to get the kids up. Allow yourself time to fully wake, sinking into God's words. Then see how your actions change the foster child's day.

Going Deeper in Scripture: Proverbs 22:6; 1 Timothy 3:4; Proverbs 24:3-4

Your Thoughts

_____

_____

_____

_____

_____

_____

_____

_____

_____

_____

_____

_____

_____

_____

_____

_____

_____

Building a
Foundation

9
God's Purpose

"And we know that in all things God works for the good of those who love him, who have been called according to his purpose."
-Romans 8:28

As a leader in a recovery program, I expected to hear similar stories to mine. I had been codependent and an enabler of an alcoholic family member. I was there to support others as they learned to cope with someone's addiction, too.

The group of ten women instead began to talk about the sexual abuse they grew up with. In most cases, it happened while their parents were high during a party. With little experience in that area, I had lots to discover from these women. Late in life, they were still dealing with the effects of hurt, pain, low self-worth, depression, and unforgiveness.

The knowledge I learned from them would later put me in a position to help heal a small, fragile life.

When God places your foster child with you, He knows your weaknesses, strengths, and heart. He chooses you to do this amazing work, knowing where you will fail and where you will succeed. He uses this relationship to teach and develop you along with the child. He pushes your limits and helps you to reach deeper than you ever thought possible. He is a God of miracles.

God has placed you for this time and purpose. He will use you to help His child. In Job 42:2, it states, "I know that you can do all things; no purpose of yours can be thwarted." God is all-powerful. He knows the past, present, and future. He knows why He chose you, even when you feel like you are not following Him or fulfilling your call as well as you should. You cannot stop His objective.

When you feel like your words failed your foster child, God can turn those words into a whole different meaning. It is like when you hear a sermon. The sermon speaks to you in a personal manner, but if you share your insight with someone else, they may have heard something different. God is still using you even when you feel incompetent. Do not give up. God sees the completed work beyond this moment.

God created us uniquely to be foster parents. Not everyone is designed to do this. He gave us the ability to love beyond ourselves through His Holy Spirit. Through that Spirit, God provides us with discernment, wisdom, and compassion to complete the work He prepared for us in advance. When you are weak, know He will get you through. Pray. Seek out others who can give you good advice. Do not fall into the trap of believing you are self-sufficient. None of us are. Be open to other opinions but be led by God.

Father, we know You have put us here for your purpose to be used for Your will. We may not always see it, but we do not have to. We recognize You see all things, know all things, and provide all things for Your greater plan, which encompasses all lives, not just ours. Help us to be open to Your direction. Give us the moment-by-moment wisdom, knowledge, and heart to take the next single step. Develop us spiritually, mentally, and physically so we can become closer to You. We love and praise You in all things. Amen

Fostering the Heart Action

Look up Bible verses about God's plans. Write down what you believe foster parents do and the limitations you have. Be honest. Look for areas of weakness and strength. When you come across an area of weakness, reach out to someone who can help, or research ways to strengthen your knowledge. Put a plan in place so you can be successful as a foster parent. When you come upon a specific foster care issue that you feel like you lack the resources to cope with, turn it over to God in prayer and allow Him to lead you.

Going Deeper in Scripture: Proverbs 19:21; Ephesians 2:10; Isaiah 46:10-11

Your Thoughts

_____

_____

_____

_____

_____

_____

_____

_____

_____

_____

_____

_____

_____

_____

_____

_____

_____

_____

_____

10
Know Your Weakness

"For the Spirit God gave us does not make us timid, but gives us power, love and self-discipline."

-2 Timothy 1:7

When we received our foster children, I knew they would initially need extra attention, love, and structure. They came from a tough situation. I thought I was prepared.

Those first months were hard. I wanted to give up, but I knew God had placed these children with us. I never doubted that. Thankfully, my husband was a rock. Leaning on him counterbalanced the stress. Our relationship grew stronger as we worked together to resolve problems.

The kids scrambled for attention, never giving me a break. Each moment felt like another crisis. By the end of the day, I was exhausted physically and mentally.

On those draining days, the last thing I wanted to do was make dinner. McDonald's sounded good. There was a bonus too: The kids would eat without a fight. As self-feeders, they learned to eat junk whenever they wanted. Establishing regular eating times with homecooked, organic food was a tough sell. As an Adult, I felt the same way but have seen the benefits of heathy eating. The kids did not.

I am not a picky eater, especially if I don't have to cook. Add to this fact that I consume more food when stressed, and the circumstances are in place to add twenty-five pounds to my body. My weakness is food. Yours may be alcohol, too much television, escaping into a cell phone, working extra hours, or a project which you make a priority. These are all ways to mentally run away from life simply to avoid the chaos.

We acquire our harmful coping skills over our lifetime. We try a little of this or that and it flourishes until it has control over our thoughts. With God's help, we can overcome the items holding us hostage. Self-discipline comes through small actions which you can start today. Putting in the time now will produce long-term results.

When our foster children first come to us, we want to make up for their situations by giving them things they never had. It is easy to provide excessive comfort, special treats, and experiences, like vacations, movies, or events. In tiny amounts, it is ok. But when we overindulge the children, they can become locked into a life of wanting. Filling their desires with objects, attention grabbing, and addictions which will never be enough. As for me, with food, we do not want the children to have to deal with these problems for the rest of their lives. Treat them like any other child, so that they can heal.

A caution: when it was decided not to return the children to their birth home, all the attention from advocates, lawyers, and caseworkers were removed. The kids wondered where all the people went. It added to their abandonment issues. We, foster parents, must be the stable piece in their lives and not add to the confusion of feeling unloved.

Trust your instincts and recognize your weaknesses. Give the children only what they need, and you can provide. Ask God for guidance. He will strengthen you, provide wisdom, and keep you healthy.

> *Father, aid us to see to the needs of the children beyond worldly standards. We recognize they are precious gifts. Show us how to make them strong not timid. Let us be examples of self-discipline. When we are weak, uplift our spirits and let us overcome. Only with Your wisdom can we manage all the situations which arise. Amen.*

Fostering the Heart Action

This week when stress builds, take a fifteen-minute breather, pray for wisdom, then go back to the challenge in front of you. If you need more of a substantial break, there are alternatives from having a volunteer take over the driving for appointments to respite weekends. What you are doing is worth it. It will pay off eventually. Stand firm God has you. You are helping to change a culture.

Going Deeper in Scripture: 1Peter 5:7; Psalm 73:26; Isaiah 40:29

Your Thoughts

_____

_____

_____

_____

_____

_____

_____

_____

_____

_____

_____

_____

_____

_____

_____

_____

_____

11

Be Courageous

"He withdrew about a stone's throw beyond them, knelt down and prayed. 'Father, if you are willing, take this cup from me; yet not my will, but yours be done.' An angel from heaven appeared to him and strengthened him. And being in anguish, he prayed more earnestly, and his sweat was like drops of blood falling to the ground."

-Luke 22:41-44

Stepping into the court room, dread of the unknown held her tongue silent. The trial went on, one witness after another. Today would make a dramatic difference in the lives of her foster children.

An invisible line was drawn down from the center of the room. Expressions from doubt to certainty peppered the audience's faces. The kids' lawyer beckoned them to sit near her. The lawyer was counting on her participation, but she wanted no part of the proceedings. Her role seemed insignificant. She only-had to describe how the kids were doing. It would not change the outcome of the events. The decision had already been made by the parent's own incriminating words, but it allowed the person sitting in orange to know how the parent's actions impacted the children they professed to love.

As she stood before the judge, her hands shook, and her voice quaked. It took courage only God could supply.

Sometimes I forget how far the layers of hurt go for our foster children. Fear can be a good motivator not to do something stupid, but it can also trap us, making it impossible to move forward. As our foster children heal, we believe the fear leaves them, until something happens. It can be a small thing with great significance.

For one of our little ones, it was a long overdue short vacation my husband and I took alone. We needed time to rest. The children were going to stay with two different families. One child was staying with a school friend, so we knew the child would have fun. While there, the child acted out. When I spoke to the child, they said, "I know it doesn't make sense, but the last time I was told I was only leaving for two weeks, I never went home." I was able to reassure the child, and after talking it through, the behavior mellowed out over the course of the day.

Have you ever had a dream where you froze, unable to move a muscle because of terror? That is when fear has control over you.

When we were asked to take in foster children as an emergency placement, I was not comfortable becoming a foster parent, but I believed if you loved a kid everything would be alright. Fear of the unknown could have blocked me from helping these beautiful children.

Jesus asked God to take away the punishment placed unfairly on His shoulders. Jesus knew what was required of Him, but that did not make it miraculously easy. Jesus was fully God and fully man. With His human side, He felt all we feel. God sent an angel to comfort and strengthen Him. Jesus will do the same for us.

Be courageous. God will provide opportunities to serve Him in ways you never considered. Fear wants to cause us to stumble. The enemy of our soul uses it to lie to us. If evil can keep us from utilizing God's power, it wins. We must stay firm in our resolve. Trust in God and instruct the children in our care to do the same.

Father, we pray that we never allow anxiety to keep us from doing Your work, or let it prevent us from enjoying all aspects of the life You give us. Help us to see opportunities instead of the impossibilities. Help us feel the Holy Spirit's power that You gave us so we can do all things through You. We need You to empower us, so we will be free of the bondage fear has over our lives. Amen.

Fostering the Heart Action

Make a list of past events when you've felt a task was impossible. How did God see you through those things? What were the results? God uses those things to grow us and glorify Him. Keep this list and add to it over time as examples of your courage and faith.

Going Deeper in Scripture: 1 Corinthians 16:13-14; Deuteronomy 31:6; 1 Chronicles 28:20

Your Thoughts

_____

_____

_____

_____

_____

_____

_____

_____

_____

_____

_____

_____

_____

_____

_____

_____

_____

12
Sacrificial Love

"Greater love has no one than this: to lay down one's life for one's friends."

-John 15:13

A friend serving the homeless in a large metropolitan area stated, "never tell the homeless you love them." I did not understand the statement until she explained, "Love on the streets means to have sex." It is not an invitation, but a demand. The misconception of what true love is stems from their pasts.

Twenty-one to fifty percent (Youth.gov, n.d.) of homeless are from the foster care system. A quarter of foster children age out of the system without family or friends to support them in the transition. Every time the child switches placement the likelihood of homelessness increases.

Foster children come to us without an understanding of real love. They have been abused, abandoned, and given confusing contradictions and unhealthy expressions of love. They were taught there are conditions which need to be met before being loved in return.

God calls us to love based on the sacrificial love of Jesus. He physically died for us, so we could have eternal life. A hard example to live up to.

First Corinthians 13 gives a definition of love. It is patient, kind, always protects, trusts, and keeps no records of wrong. The homes foster kids come from express the opposite. There is envy, shame, ignorance, anger, self-service, or evil behavior. They learn love fails constantly and is unpredictable.

With consistency, we are the examples of unconditional love, which is giving and not expecting anything in return. We lay our lives aside to help someone. I believe that is the definition of being a foster parent. Love is not a warm fuzzy feeling in the pit of your stomach. It is the choice you make in your daily actions. When we unselfishly direct our time and energy toward another human being instead of ourselves.

How do we implement this in our lives with foster children? Start with listening. This will teach you who these kids are and how to relate to them. It will give you clues to their characteristics, both good and bad, which will allow you to better understand their needs.

It will take energy, time, and sacrificial love to help them heal, grow, and become all they can be. There will be times when you must put your desires away to focus on theirs and do it without resentment. This can only be done through the grace of God.

Foster children come with little notice. They do not come at convenient times when we can plan perfect conditions. They get placed into our lives wherever we are. For us to incorporate them into our family, we had to rearrange a planned vacation, buy furniture and clothing, and get them into the dentist while working full-time. How we handled all this was our first expression of love to these kids.

Laying down our lives encourages *them*, even when *we* are discouraged. Giving them the first fruits of our labor is another example. Buying them new pants and patching the hole in our own. Or when they behave badly, and we discipline their actions but choose not to allow it to affect our feelings towards them.

Showing children God-filled love not only helps heal their brokenness but is an example to others working with social services. We give foster kids unconditional love when they have not earned it because God first loved us.

Lord, assist us to set aside our own selfish wants and desires, so we will love, understand, and have patience toward the children we protect. Guide us to know when to reach out and pull back so the kids may heal and flourish. Thank You for the opportunity to see Your love in action. Today we pray for encouragement, so we may stand strong against the evil of this world and proclaim Your love defeats it all. Amen.

Fostering the Heart Action

Help your foster child recognize healthy love by pointing it out when you see it. When someone does something unselfishly, praise them.

Going Deeper in Scripture: 1 Corinthians 13; John 13:34-35; James 2:8

Your Thoughts

_____

_____

_____

_____

_____

_____

_____

_____

_____

_____

_____

_____

_____

_____

_____

_____

_____

13
Who to Trust

"The Lord is with me; I will not be afraid.
What can mere mortals do to me?
The Lord is with me; he is my helper.
I look in triumph on my enemies.
It is better to take refuge in the Lord than to trust in humans."

-Psalm 118:6-8

The highway flagger raised his stop sign in front of my SUV. As I waited, I glanced in my rearview mirror to see a front-end loader heading toward my car. His bucket lifted preventing his view of me at the base of the hill. I looked up at the flagger, but he stood directly in my path. There was no place for me to move. I turned my wheel and honked my horn hoping not to kill the construction worker. The hit came with screeching metal and the jarring of my bones. The driver stopped immediately.

When we get into our cars, we assume we will make it to our destination safely. That did not happen. My car was smashed, and I received bumps and bruises.

No one expects to be in an accident. We follow the set rules for traffic safety. But in the United States, there are over six million auto accidents a year. I was only one of them. We put our blind faith in human institutions of federal regulations to keep us protected. Yet the Lord is our greatest asset. He is our helper and we do not need to be afraid when He is on our side. Many find it difficult to trust in the Bible God gave us to live by. We question Him and the Bible while accepting man-made rules every day. I was blessed to see God's presence through small miracles, and visiting Israel where history can be seen.

God prepared my husband and I well before He asked us to take in traumatized children. He taught us to trust Him through smaller challenges, then built up our trust through bigger and bigger asks. It started with giving strangers rides in this crazy world where you do not know what type of person they may be. Next, we spent our limited savings leading a mission trip. Not an easy task when the prior year we'd faced foreclosure. God then sent my husband to college for the first time at the age of 35. Every time we stepped out God was present, providing for our needs even through the difficulties.

He used our experience and personal struggle to develop a faith-filled, everlasting relationship with Him. Because of the foundation God formed, we were able to say yes and stand firm in our decision to take on the kids even without foster care training, preparation, or prior knowledge of the children. God aligned our path with His purpose. It required us to trust Him daily. When we feel like we are getting nowhere and there is no end in sight, it can feel overwhelming, especially when the children act out or plans go against our desires.

Children are born open, loving, and trusting. They assume adults will protect, provide, and care for them, but foster children discover over time this is not true. Their experience influences how they react. We must show them we are dependable before they will let us in. This takes time. As a foster parent, we need to teach that it is ok to open ourselves to believe in others, but with discernment of what or who is trustworthy.

Bible reading and prayer can help us see others as God does. When God tugs on your heart to move you toward action, respond in obedience even when you do not understand. Trust Him to pull the small pieces together for big results.

Father, I pray that today we will search for and listen to Your voice. Teach us to gain faith through the small things. Where we have our own stumbling blocks because of past mistakes or regrets, remove their influence, so we can walk in Your footsteps unencumbered by things that hold us back from becoming all we can become. Help us to submit to Your teachings, not fight them. Let us be the first to be trustworthy to others, and when we are hurt, restore us, and help us to let it go. Amen.

Fostering the Heart Action

Help build your foster children's trust by example. Take an interest in what's important to them, promise to do it with them, then follow through. If you cannot do something they have asked, tell them, and stick to it even when they pester you. Being repetitive will teach them your words are true.

Going Deeper in Scripture: Jeremiah 17:7-8; 2 Corinthians 5:7; Isaiah 31:1; Psalm 56:3-5

Your Thoughts

_____

_____

_____

_____

_____

_____

_____

_____

_____

_____

_____

14
A Father's Sin

"Our ancestors sinned and are no more,
and we bear their punishment."

-Lamentations 5:7

Children are resilient. How many times have you heard that comforting phrase? I've heard it every time someone is getting a divorce, when a child enters foster care, or when a parent has done something which hurts their child, whether inadvertently or selfishly.

Society likes to believe children will bounce back from harsh words, a heavy fist, or absenteeism of a parent. Because the children of America don't commit suicide, take drugs, or become promiscuous, they're resilient. (I write that sarcastically.)

The after-effects of what children have been through because of parental abuse (or abuse from other sources) last a lifetime. We can put bandages on them to heal the scab, but the pain will affect them every time they come to a new phase in growing up, like when they first start to date, when they get married, or upon having children.

Foster children are not responsible for what their family members have done, but they do have to deal with the consequences of those actions. They may have picked up bad habits, feel alone, live with fear, or become vulnerable to predators. We have our work cut out for us to help teach these children and to do our part to reverse the damage done. Children do not have the tools to combat the problems around them. Through counseling, interaction with us, and the courts' protective decisions, the children will begin to learn how to deal with their emotions and hurts.

The effects of our ancestor's sins do change a child's life, perspective, and coping mechanisms. We all need to recognize that our actions affect those around us and the next generation. If we can stop bad behaviors before they start, we have nothing to deal with.

Pay attention to your actions today. Watch how others react to them. Be honest with yourself and adjust behaviors which are not helpful. Read the Bible. It is full of stories of how one person, for good or bad, changed the course of their lives. David's affair with Bathsheba ended in murder, rebelliousness, pain, jealousy, and death of an infant. God forgave David when he repented, but the damage to lives had already done.

As adults, we should have the discipline to be constructive in our behaviors. We cannot change every mistake we ever made or fix all the things kids go through, but we can give them the same love God shows us and equip them to deal with the hurt caused by their prior experiences. We can stand up for them, provide mental health care, and teach them how to protect themselves. We can lead them to the healing grace of God.

Our foster children can blossom despite the damage of their past with our aid. Show them how to use their upbringing to strengthen their futures, love unconditionally, help others in similar situations, and teach them how to embrace all of who they are. God uses our biggest hurts to mature us into better people. Let your children know they are strong, incredible, powerful, and capable of doing anything with God.

> *Lord, we pray for you to use us as Your instruments of grace. Cover over the multitudes of mistakes we, as parents, have made. Forgive us. Let our children not carry that burden but let them heal and give them peace. Show us when to be strong and stand up for those who cannot stand up for themselves. Teach us to love as You do. Amen.*

Fostering the Heart Action

If you are tempted to make an excuse for a behavior today, whether yours or another's, stop and consider instead how you can change your actions to bring a positive resolution. An apology or acknowledgment can go a long way to reestablishing a good relationship. If we take an extra five minutes working slowly through a problem, it can help deter a half hour dealing with the mental breakdown of a traumatized child when they cannot handle a confrontation or frustration. Patience and gentleness are the key here.

Going Deeper in Scripture: 2 Samuel 11 and 12; Romans 7:14-20; Romans 8:5

Your Thoughts

_____

_____

_____

_____

_____

_____

_____

_____

_____

_____

_____

_____

_____

15
The Smallest Seed

"The kingdom of heaven is like a mustard seed, which a man took and planted in his field. Though it is the smallest of all seeds, yet when it grows, it is the largest of garden plants and becomes a tree, so that the birds come and perch in its branches."
-Matthew 13:31-32

Working with human services, lawyers, and courts can become frustrating. Each agency has an agenda and a point of view. One group may want one specific counselor or approach taken within a case, while another believes something else would be better.

As a foster parent, we feel we know what is best for the kids in our care. Sometimes agencies hide their purposes for the decisions they make. We can begin to feel like a pawn in a chess game, confused about who to believe.

I recall one specific family meeting that was particularly trying for me. It appeared the team overseeing the case was favoring return to home even though the parent had yet to complete any of the tasks assigned them, had not changed their behaviors, and was uncertain of their ability to parent.

I wanted to say, "if you are going to return the kids to their parent, just do it, so I can get on with my life." But then God nudged me, and my husband spoke gently reminding me of how much better the kids were doing. It had been a year, and they had begun to heal. I realized, as I stilled myself to listen to God's whispers, that it did not matter how much longer we had the children. What was important was that we used every day with them as a gift.

It was our blessing to show God's love by helping the children discover, flourish, and heal in a healthy home.

Moments make a difference. When I see our foster kids with heartfelt smiles, being kind to one another, or doing what we asked them the first time, I know we have encouraged changes which will affect their entire life. It's priceless watching our little ones pray, sing Christian songs, and happily get ready to go to church. These seeds planted in their hearts lead toward eternity with Jesus. It will affect their future families, too. They will be better parents, friends, and spouses.

When you plant a mustard seed, you provide a firm foundation and stability your foster child can learn to trust. When you water and nurture the seed, it sprouts new growth, then shoots off into many branches—branches of peace, kindness, joy, self-esteem, and self-control. These lead to a healthier life for your foster kid and provides a place for future family to perch.

Do you remember a time when a small act displayed the love of Christ to you and planted a seed of faith? We are the planters of these children. Our words and actions will not come back empty but will accomplish God's goals. Together, we can effect a positive change to brighten the future of the children placed in our lives.

So, when things are not going as you hoped, when circumstances appear to spiral out of control, don't let it devour you into nothingness or tempt you to quit. In the years to come, the agencies, counselors, and advocates will drift away. The consistency you develop with your foster children will be the root of their future. Sink into God's loving embrace and allow Him to use you to show unconditional love.

> *Dear Lord, I pray for encouragement for those of us who feel we don't have much time left to help grow these young lives into strong saplings. Give us daily grace, peace, and assurance we are accomplishing Your goal. God, open our eyes. Let us see what a single moment can do to bring transformation in the lives of those around us. We know that You have a perfect plan. Help us to put our faith in You. Amen.*

Fostering the Heart Action

Take your foster children to a park. Find an animal or bird and teach them how God provides for all its needs: food, water, and fur/feathers which protect. Then remind them God will take care of them as well. This can be tricky because of their current and past life but give them the hope they need.

Going Deeper in Scripture: Isaiah 55:10-11, Galatians 6:7-8, 2 Corinthians 9:6

Your Thoughts

_____

_____

_____

_____

_____

_____

_____

_____

_____

_____

_____

_____

_____

_____

_____

_____

16
Finding Rest

"Come to Me, all who are weary and heavy-laden, and I will give you rest."

-Matthew 11:28

There are days when I pry open my eyes, look around the bedroom, and think, "Do I really have to get up?" What I want is to bury under the covers and sleep. Let's face it: sometimes we are mentally and physically exhausted. On those days, I remind myself we are blessed.

Imagine what it was like for American pioneers. They faced miles of travel in wagons over bumpy roads, never sure if they would live through the next river crossing or snowstorm. Finding rest on beds of blankets stuffed between wooden crates. Rising, they lit a fire, then heated water which they hauled from a stream, and cooked a few precious coffee beans. They did not have the luxury of saying, "What a rough night. I think I'll lay around and catch up with the wagon train tomorrow."

I wake up with soft, clean blankets on a comfy mattress, in a home with a warm, toasty heater, and the drifting smell of hot coffee, as my preprogramed pot turns itself on. When I run low on supplies, I drive five minutes to the store and buy what I need.

Why did the settlers live like they did? Were they stronger than we are today? Maybe it is simply that they had no choice. They had children to feed, jobs to do, and had to take care of their physical and mental needs. Just like we do.

God existed yesterday, today, and tomorrow. His promises are always true. He tells us to come to Him when we are weary, to lay down our heavy burdens, and that when we do, He will fill us with spiritual and physical rest. On mornings when you are not sure how you can pull yourself up and start a new day, take one step at a time and lean into the Lord. He will wrap you in His toasty embrace and carry you through.

Foster children add extra challenges which can be hard to face. If you are exhausted, ask your spouse to cover some of your duties or create a buffer. This could be taking the kids to a movie, their attention captured for a blessed two hours. Depending on your children's independence level, they may be able to play outside to give you an hour of quiet. In some cases, playgrounds, swimming pools, libraries, and computer time can be structured so you are overseeing the activity, but not participating in it, or only minimally. This allows you to get some level of relaxation.

It's important to recognize when you need self-care. John 4:6 tells us that even Jesus wearied from his travels and rested by a well. Plan on working restorative rest for yourself into your schedule.

Like the pioneers, there are somethings we must do, but ask God to help you have joy in the work. My grandfather had an amazing ability to make labor fun. There was a wiener roast over an open fire during harvest time. Competitions to move stones in the field. The promise of riding minibikes or swinging on the barn loft swing after chores.

Teach your foster child the benefits of sharing household tasks. They go faster when divided. Incorporate games into the work. Chores teach self-respect, diligence, teamwork, and include the children in family. Initially it will take a bit of work to show them how, but over time it will alleviate your weariness.

> *God Almighty, we ask You to shoulder our burdens and help us release them to You. Take the weariness from our souls. Let us be good examples for our foster children, showing what it looks like when a family works together in harmony. Give us direction*

and creativity to turn work into fun. Remind us to praise our children for their efforts even when it is not done to our specifications. We know with Your direction we will learn together. Help us to build a home of rest and renewal in You. Amen.

Fostering the Heart Action

Look ahead and pick out a chore you can work together on. Find a reasonable reward for a job well done, and let the children know in advance what will happen when the job is completed. Depending on the chore, the reward could be an extra hour watching tv, or if it is a full day project, kids these days still like wiener roasts and s'mores.

Going Deeper in Scripture: Ecclesiastics 4:6; Jeremiah 31:25-28; 2 Corinthians 12:9

Your Thoughts

_____

_____

_____

_____

_____

_____

_____

_____

_____

_____

_____

17
The Harvest Is Coming

"Let us not lose heart in doing good, for in due time we will reap if we do not grow weary."

-Galatians 6:9

I looked into defiant eyes, knowing the child was testing me. Could they get away with unruly behavior this time? Today's battle had cropped up frequently over the last two years.

Sometimes, I think it would be nice to move on to a different battle just for variety. But the truth is every time this foster child sees their parent, they revert to old patterns, and my husband and I live the consequences. I remind myself that under the tough exterior, this child's security is deeply shaken each time they have a visit.

One of the issues we face as foster parents is that the schedule always changes, either more visitation with the parent, less, or sometimes none. It is up to us to smooth the path even when it disrupts our own plans. While the Department of Human Services, lawyers, and counselors figure out what is best for the parents and kids, we shower love on the children and walk beside them.

I must confess, there are moments when I become frustrated and disappointed in both the process and the people. There will be times when you stick to your beliefs and stand up for the kids. Other times, you will bow out of the fight because it is either not worth the struggle or it only causes division.

The children are watching our responses. Being the adult in this situation, we have learned over many years how to deal with feelings. The children do not have our experience, coping mechanisms, or training. When the child lives in fear, the relational part of the brain will have damage due to over exposure of cortisol. It is a natural chemical produced when we are scared. With time and intervention, it will heal.

Staying strong in doing good has produced tremendous progress in our foster children. Yes, there are still insolent moments, but these conflicts used to be daily, even hourly. Now the behavior has dropped to a few minutes or perhaps an hour at most and only on specific days. We have the privilege of helping teach the kids how to deal with the ups and downs of their relationship with their biological parent. Foster families serve as examples of how to treat and bond with others. We demonstrate how to be strong and kind, while not becoming victims in life.

Recently at dinner, my husband said, "Look around you. Do you see the families you are affecting? We are not only influencing the kids in our care, but someday their spouses and children too."

What we do as foster parents will change generations to come. If you are serving as a foster parent, do not lose heart and grow weary—you have one of the most important jobs in the world. You may not see it now, but you are changing future lives for the glory of God and the betterment of our world. Stay strong—God will reap the harvest that is coming.

> *Father God, thank You for bringing these blessings into our lives even when it becomes difficult. Lift our weariness away, giving us new strength to do good for You. We know we are tending the fields to produce a mighty harvest. We need You, Lord. As we join in lifting this prayer to You, fill us with Your peace, courage, strength, and wisdom to meet the next challenge. Please remind us of the good we are doing and help us to see beyond today to a future of hope. Amen.*

Fostering the Heart Action

Prior to the children coming home from a visit, complete any undone tasks. Put away all distractions, then pray for a calm spirit.

When the kids open the door, greet them, establish a quick transition from the parent (long goodbyes add tension), give the kids a bit of space, then spend a little time listening to them before you start them on homework, showers, or any duty. If possible, delay chores until the next day. Make the transition easy and comfortable. When the pressure is off, it takes less time before you can start their usual routine.

Going Deeper in Scripture: Philippians 4:12-13; 1 Corinthians 13:4-7; Isaiah 40:28-31

Your Thoughts

_____

_____

_____

_____

_____

_____

_____

_____

_____

_____

_____

_____

_____

_____

_____

_____

18
Beware of the Hidden Pits

"The woman said to the serpent, 'We may eat fruit from the trees in the garden, but God did say, "You must not eat fruit from the tree that is in the middle of the garden, and you must not touch it, or you will die."' 'You will not certainly die,' the serpent said to the woman. 'For God knows that when you eat from it your eyes will be opened, and you will be like God.'"

-Genesis 3:2-5

The tree-studded mountains surrounded my sister and me. We followed a winding path, sunlight bouncing off the surrounding rocks as we emerged into a boulder field.

My sister suddenly stopped short. Immediately behind her, I screeched and stumbled, inadvertently pushing her toward a crevice. She lunged sideways in a mad attempt not to land in a nest of snakes hidden in a pit just below her feet. I had not intended to use her as a barrier, but I did. Our hiking trip changed in that instant from simple, enjoyable camaraderie, to a story I will never forget.

Even with the best intentions, we can make decisions that pull our foster children away from God into a pit of serpents. We agreed to a new counselor working with the kids to help prepare them for reconciliation. It was a positive move, we thought. It took one visit for us to see the kids lose progress. They had no trust in the new therapist and felt they were carrying the burden of reconciliation. The methods used scared them and put them on the defensive, so they retreated.

The parent struggled as well. This caused the kids to become distant, have more nightmares, and return to old, unhealthy coping mechanisms. What was meant for the family's good became a trial.

If we can unintentionally push someone into a pit, how much more can we damage someone when we *follow* a serpent? Eve believed the snake when he said her eyes would be opened, and that God was holding out on her. Instead of new life, her actions caused death for humanity as they knew it. Not trusting God was a big mistake.

Foster children have enough upheaval in their lives—they do not need to be placed in the middle of conflict. Protect them from hearing things that will be hurtful to them. Keep your opinions of family members private. Voicing concerns in front of children causes them insecurity, creates divided loyalties, and places them in a position where they feel obligated to solve the situation.

As foster parents, we are given a great task. We collect information, process it, pray about it, and then determine the best direction for the children. This is not sitting back and letting others make the choices. It is using our voices to speak out. There will be serpents in the child's core group, those who will try to lead us away from God's will and what is best for the kids. Recognize their voices, then encourage movement toward God's vision. Be the advocate for your foster children.

When foster parents face choices, our first action should be to lay it before the Lord in prayer and look beyond our small sphere for His complete overview. It is easy to get swayed when we put our needs before those of the kids. There are days when we are told of a new constraint, additional staff who will be coming to our homes, or a plan which will add to our already stretched schedules. Romans 8:28 tells us God has our best interest in mind and a purpose for what is occurring. Trust Him and look beyond the moment.

> *Papa, thank You for loving us. We pray we will listen to Your voice leading us away from those who would guide us into bad decisions. Help us to know the difference. We recognize our*

influence can hurt, heal, benefit, or destroy, so we promise to give that responsibility sincere consideration. Amen

Fostering the Heart Action

If a new plan is presented, do not agree immediately. Take the time to research, pray, or get outside viewpoints. When you are sure the decision is good, then implement it.

Going Deeper in Scripture: Jeremiah 50:6; Proverbs 2:12-15; Matthew 18:6

Your Thoughts

_____

_____

_____

_____

_____

_____

_____

_____

_____

_____

_____

_____

_____

_____

_____

_____

_____

_____

When Life is Upside Down

19
Blessed in the Serving

"The Lord has established His throne in heaven,
and his kingdom rules over all.
Praise the Lord, you his angels,
you mighty ones who do his bidding,
who obey his word.
Praise the Lord, all his heavenly hosts,
you his servants who do his will."

-Psalm 103:19-21

It got harder, not easier. The first three months were crazy difficult, but they had the strength to do anything for a short while. Human Services promised the children would return home within six months. She counted down the days to when her life would go back to normal.

When the seventh month came and went with no end in sight, she crashed. She could no longer just tolerate the behavior of the children after parent visits or listen to the horrendous stories of the kids' past without screaming, "How could anyone do that to a child?"

She no longer wanted to stay silent in the family meetings that never appeared to demand change from the parent but allowed them to stay in a victim role. Especially when the group put the children through excessive counseling and intrusive visits from various professionals.

With shoulders bowed under the weight, she cried to God. *Lord, help me.* Trapped in her own world, she focused on what she had given up: The family business, time alone with her husband and children, vacations, and ministry in far off countries. All she saw was the endless laundry, cleaning bathrooms, strangers evaluating them, and the difficulties of being a parent of kids with trauma.

God answered her cry by giving her special angels. He brought someone who they could employ, allowing her to decrease her workload for their business. Her husband took over some additional care items for the kids and blessed her with a short-term housekeeper. Human services went to the courts, securing a decision to suspend visits. Friends stepped forward to help with expenses for clothing, food, and laundry detergent. Caring people prayed for them.

God is genuinely good and faithful. When we feel we can no longer go on, He surrounds us with love. God is the great provider. He will be there for you in those dark, broken moments when you don't feel like you can take another step. He has given us the greatest calling—to help heal the broken, love His children, and give them hope for a future. With this work, He gives us a shoulder to lean on, courage beyond ourselves, and His blessing. We cannot ask for more.

When it gets tough, do not think you need to do everything by yourself. Ask your case worker for respite services or help driving the foster child to appointments. Friends can help with various jobs, whether related to the children, or miscellaneous tasks. Be bold and ask them to help you.

If you are struggling, admit it. There is no shame in asking for help. If someone says no, nothing has changed. Human services have limited resources, so when you can invite a friend or family member to help serve, it only expands God's kingdom.

Do not allow yourself to become overtired, or you will be unable to do the fundamental work God wants. You may not feel like it, but you are an angel to your foster children. He will give us His mighty strength for He is sovereign overall. Rest in the knowledge that you are serving Him.

Father, today, hear the cry of our hearts. We want to be a blessing to these children. We pray for the healing of their broken innocence and that they would know the hope found in You. We ask for a bright and glorious future for them. Lord, when we can no longer do it on our own, please bring angels to help us do the work You have given us so that we may glorify You. We praise you for all things. Amen.

Fostering the Heart Action

Recognize that you are blessed and have something to give to others. Make a list of all God has provided you over your lifetime. It could be health, family, work, a smile, or a helping hand. Take a few minutes every morning before you rise to remember, worship, and praise God for all He has given you.

Going Deeper in Scripture: Psalm 150:1-6; Psalm 34:2; Habakkuk 3:17-18

Your Thoughts

_____

_____

_____

_____

_____

_____

_____

_____

_____

_____

_____

20
When Life Happens

"…who keeps an oath even when it hurts,
and does not change their mind….
Whoever does these things will never be shaken."
-Psalm 15:4-5

Foster parents can plan for the addition of a child. We can rearrange a room with an additional bed, make a trip to the store for extra clothing, and set up provisions for the kid to attend school. We prepare our hearts and minds for the acceptance of a new family member. But what happens when the unexpected comes along?

My husband was in a bad motorcycle accident. It was traumatic for our family. Emotions were high, I had no replacement at work, and our foster kids needed even more focused care and attention since their world was upset. The man who protected them from the bad people of their past laid in a hospital bed far from home.

I called in my family for help, organizing everyone's roles one day at a time. It was hard for me to even think, but God gave me an outward calm and helped me to work with all the different personalities.

My adult daughters and my brother-in-law took turns sitting with my husband when I was at work. Our older children rotated watching their foster siblings. My 80-year-old parents came to help prepare meals and transport the children. When the family could not be with my foster children, friends picked them up and fed them dinner. The church set up a meal train. We were showered in prayer. All this tangible help provided by God kept me from being shaken.

It never occurred to me to call human services, advocates, or birth parents. When we promised to take in our foster kids, we took an oath to raise them as long as needed. There were no stipulations for a return. They were a part of our family, and the family pulls together when times are hard.

Several days after the accident, I took the little ones to visit my husband in the hospital. I shared with them what to expect—the oxygen, the tubes, and the brokenness of his right side.

Standing in the hospital hallway, the middle child was quiet. "Are you ok?" I asked. No reply. "Do you want to go in to see him?" A nod yes. I gave them a quick hug and we walked toward the door.

Entering his room, the children quickly skirted the bed to his good side. Each in turn stroked his arm, murmuring words of missing him and asking if he would be okay. Reassured, they soon started to investigate all the machines and equipment. My husband and I calmly answered each question.

As we entered my husband's private bathroom, the middle child leaned into my side. This kid is an internal processor, so instead of words, this is the move they make when their world is rocked. This child needs simple touch and understanding. It brought tears to my eyes. I realized how unsure the kids had been. Their relief was tangible.

Afterwards in the car, they all talked for a few minutes, but soon fell asleep, another indicator of their stress. These kids don't take naps—ever.

God do not let our minds waiver but help us to remain firm. Thank You for strengthening us to keep our oath to raise Your children. I am grateful You have made us a family. You are our strength and rock. The provider of peace, calm, and joy amid troubles. I pray we will lean into You as strongly today as we did during our trial. Never let us forget the importance of Your daily provision, so that we will never be shaken. Amen.

Fostering the Heart Action

We never expect emergencies. Take the time to discuss with your spouse what will happen in case of a major trial. Put back up plans in place. Who will watch the children if you cannot? Make sure to include a contingency for dealing with the foster children's emotions.

Going Deeper in Scripture: Matthew 5:37; Deuteronomy 23:21-23; Proverbs 20:25

Your Thoughts

_____

_____

_____

_____

_____

_____

_____

_____

_____

_____

_____

_____

_____

_____

_____

_____

_____

21
The Intimate Act of Prayer

"And pray in the Spirit on all occasions with all kinds of prayers and requests. With this in mind, be alert and always keep on praying for all the Lord's people."

-Ephesians 6:18

Snuggled in bed, the ringing phone jarred us awake. Our child's voice shook, "I hit a patch of ice in the canyon. My car slid off the road and plunged into the river." The cell phone crackled and died.

Service is horrible in the mountains. My husband called the police. They were sending an ambulance. Our foster children slept in their beds, unaware of the events. My husband jumped in the car and drove down the mountain in search of our child, while I waited for word. In the dark hours, I prayed. I felt helpless.

It is easy to downplay the importance of prayer. We want to do something more tangible, more proactive. I would have preferred to rush to my child so I could wrap them in my arms, but, with sleeping foster children at home, I instead was called to fulfill the vital role of prayer.

God hears our cries. He knows our desperate pleas. As a parent, waiting to hear the unknown can be overwhelming. When we are weak, Romans 8:26 tells us the Spirit will help us and intercedes with wordless groans when we do not know how to pray.

Prayer is an intimate act of conversing with God. Revelation 5:8 says, "…Each one had a harp and they were holding golden bowls full of incense, which are the prayers of God's people."

I envision the aroma of our thoughts and words rising to the sky, enveloping God in a swirling mass of mist. It is an honor—we are blessed to touch God in this manner. It should not be considered the default, last, or only thing we can contribute because we are not there in person to do more. Prayer is vital to our relationship with Jesus. The word prayer is used 367 times in the NIV Bible and is referenced much more. Prayer is important to God.

Not only are we called to pray, but to do so on all occasions, whether we are happy or sad. So, how do you pray throughout the day? Be alert, so you can continually send up silent, small prayers over situations as they occur, rather than waiting until bedtime or when it is convenient. It is a discipline that allows our focus to turn toward God first instead of as an afterthought. We invite Him into our hearts and minds whether we are excited to see a triumph our foster child accomplished, or we're sad because they have been hurt.

When we go for an extended period without seeing an answer to a particular prayer, we can believe the conversation is useless and stop. That is when we rely on the knowledge of God's nature we learn through the Bible. We trust Him to answer when it is time. Sometimes He answers, but we do not like it or do not see it. Ask God to let you see through His eyes so you may understand, or to give you grace to accept His answer when you really do not want to.

My foster children expressed it like this:

- We pray to thank Him.
- We pray to have a better life.
- And we pray because we love Him.

There is nothing insignificant about that.

God, we pray You might allow us a glimpse of answered prayer today. That we would recognize the privilege You have given us to be a part of Your work. And may we listen to all You say during our intimate conversations. We thank You and praise You. Amen.

Fostering the Heart Action

Before you say a word tomorrow morning, pray. Open the lines of communication with God so the conversation can follow you through the day. Prayer is a simple sharing of your thoughts and feelings with God. If you need a good starting point, look at Matthew 6:8-13.

Going Deeper in Scripture: Philippians 4:6-7; 1 John 5:14; Jeremiah 29:12

Your Thoughts

_____
_____
_____
_____
_____
_____
_____
_____
_____
_____
_____
_____
_____
_____
_____

22
Grumbling a Timewaster

"Don't grumble against one another, brothers and sisters, or you will be judged. The Judge is standing at the door!"

-James 5:9

The meeting inched along slower than an ice cube melting in a freezer. For every decision made, a new discussion item came up. A groan slipped from my lips, as the one person who always takes the group on a tangent asked a totally irrelevant question. I glanced at the clock. Another half hour of my life devoured by inconsequential topics not helpful to the children. A team of twelve people discussing their future, and by default, mine too.

Another home visit. What's that make, four this month? Don't they know I need to work, clean the house, pick up the kids, do homework, cook dinner, and a thousand other things?

These thoughts are a steady stream of waste. How much time do you typically spend complaining? 5 minutes? An hour? The entire day? It is time you can never get back.

I know there are occasions when I just want to be a regular family. Bring the kids home after school, chill out for a bit, then do homework and dinner, with time to relax after baths. Aw, what a beautiful dream. But we all have commitments and work with people whose viewpoint contradicts our own. We can do nothing to change those circumstances.

Protesting will not get a job done faster or create an atmosphere of love. It may add obstacles or walls that cannot be climbed. In family court, it can distract from the valid point you are trying to make. The judge can look at you as disruptive. Wait patiently and use wisdom when to speak.

Grumbling can happen under our breath, aloud, or even just in our thoughts. No matter how we express it, each way leads to the same result. Complaining tears down ourselves and those around us. It builds irritability, discord, and slows down the process of accomplishing a task. It is a tool of the enemy to destroy relationships and hearts.

God has given us the power to control our reactions. We can be attentive, helpful, and hold on to a positive attitude. Trust God to lead and pray for His intervention when necessary. We are a small portion of the whole picture. Only God sees all the parts. He knows why and how each person will be used in a specific time and place. Sometimes He uses the frustrating people or circumstances to challenge the way we think, to open our eyes to an unfamiliar perspective, or to refine our abilities.

God is the only being who can judge. He sees the inner thoughts and heart of a person, including our own. He chooses the consequences for our actions. When we grumble about others, the Bible tells us we will be judged as we have judged. I do not want to stand before the Lord knowing I have treated others unfairly.

Dear Lord in Heaven, You are the Almighty Power, the Creator of all. We cannot see into the hearts and minds of others, but You can. So, we leave them up to You. We can only be responsible for our own actions. So, let us start with ourselves, help us to see what we need to change within us. When we need to be quiet and wait, give us patience. But when we need to speak, give us kind words. Help us to see those around us as You do. In Jesus' name, amen.

Fostering the Heart Action

When your day is not going how you would want, stop, and remember all the blessings before you. Start with the simple things, like a beautiful day or a kind stranger who opened a door. Then make a conscious decision to be a part of brightening someone else's day with an act of kindness. Focusing outward instead of inward will help you to change your perspective. The smile you receive from others will fill your soul at the same time as uplifting them.

Going Deeper in Scripture: Philippians 2:14-15; Exodus 16:8-9; Luke 6:37

Your Thoughts

_____

_____

_____

_____

_____

_____

_____

_____

_____

_____

_____

_____

_____

_____

_____

_____

_____

23
Waiting Expectantly

"In the morning, Lord, you hear my voice;
in the morning I lay my request before you
and wait expectantly."

-Psalm 5:3

Firing up my computer was a new experience today. It struggled to ignite. Yesterday, it popped right on, no problem. But this morning it was slow and plodding. My expectations for its performance went unmet.

Expectations are assumptions we make when we want our wishes or desires to be met. I have been struggling with what I expect of life and others. I believe my foster children should do what I ask them the first time without a fight. I hope my husband will heal from his motorcycle accident overnight. I envision authoring a great novel which will help mature new adults in faith.

Unfortunately, our reality is that the foster children do not respond until I have repeated myself three or four times. My husband's ribs have decided not to fuse together yet. Instead of books which will spur on a new generation, I fill my blog with devotions.

On occasion, things run smoothly. I get exactly what I plan, but the results still seem lacking. I expected to feel satisfaction, but instead I remain wondering if there is more to accomplish. Was my vision not grand enough? Maybe God had better plans and I let Him down.

God invites us into a journey with Him. We cannot sidestep the track He's set up. Trusting Him to sustain and direct us will lead us into God's expectations for our lives.

When we follow our false desires, we miss out on all the possibilities of the current day. The result can be unrest, unfulfillment, and unwillingness. It can lead to anger and disrespect, blocking us from seeing and being all God intended. If we live for what *will* happen instead of the present, time passes without accomplishing the purpose God *currently* has for us. We need to align our will with God's to meet our full potential.

Years ago, I felt hopeless. Our electricity was going to be turned off due to nonpayment. I just wanted to jump ahead in time for our next paycheck. The day before this was to occur, we received a refund check from an old car insurance policy for the amount we needed to pay the utility bill. Only God could cause an insurance company to give us money from a closed account. He used this moment to teach me dependence and show answered prayer. God provides precisely what we require when we need it.

He does not owe us our wants. He sets us where we are for His purpose, plan, and timing. The question is: *am I doing all He wants?*

When we do not see the big overall plan but only a tiny part, we can become discouraged. James 1:6-8 says, "But when you ask, you must believe and not doubt, because the one who doubts is like a wave of the sea, blown and tossed by the wind. That person should not expect to receive anything from the Lord. Such a person is double-minded and unstable in all they do." Stand firm in your faith. Open yourself to see His desires, and to give you the ability to envision His greater purpose. Don't miss the blessings of the work God is doing in your life. Instead wait expectantly for God's secrets to unfold.

> *Father God, help us to put away our expectations. We do not want them to be barriers to You and Your will. Help us to stay in the moment and appreciate this day. Don't let us miss the opportunities You give us. We wait to see You do more than we can imagine. Thank You, God, and praise You for this moment. In Jesus' name, amen.*

Fostering the Heart Action

Review your current expectations of your life circumstances and the people around you. Are they in line with God, reasonable, beneficial to more than yourself? If you answer yes to these questions, then look at the goal through God's perspective to gain new vision. If you answer no, perhaps it is time to shift your priorities. Follow His direction and be patient.

Going Deeper in Scripture: James 1:2-8; 12 Proverbs 16:9; Jeremiah 29:11

Your Thoughts

_____

_____

_____

_____

_____

_____

_____

_____

_____

_____

_____

_____

_____

24

Resentment is not Pretty

"Since, then, you have been raised with Christ, set your hearts on things above, where Christ is, seated at the right hand of God. Set your minds on things above, not on earthly things."
-Colossians 3:1-2

The kids returned from their parental visit carrying new toys, a common occurrence. Our foster child mentioned the need for their parent to find a place to live.

One of the kids suggested I give them our rental property. My mind lit up like a bottle rocket. Are you joking? We have worked hard all our lives to get what we have. We make payments on that house, pay for electricity, insurance, property tax, etc.

The child did not realize any of this. My mind translated this conversation into, it's not enough I am raising the children. Now I am supposed to be responsible for the birth parent too.

What spilled out of my mouth, I am not proud of. I reminded the child I worked full-time for what I had, besides cleaning clothes, cooking meals, and scrubbing bathrooms. "And now you want me to give your parent a house too?"

It took only a moment for remorse to hit me.

I struggle with handling all the daily responsibilities while my foster children's biological parent picks them up for playtime. You may struggle with a parent who avoids hard emotions. Or visitations that overlap a school project or commitments the child has, but the bio parent does not get it done. There are also the bio parents who go absent for a time. It could be a week or two months. If you feel you or the children are being treated unfairly, you may react poorly.

Our strong emotions toward biological parent(s) cannot impact our parenting of our foster children. What we do is *for the kids*, so they may become healthy individuals and have a positive relationship with their biological parents.

Resentment is not a pretty thing. It makes our hearts callous. The dictionary[1] says resentment is "a feeling of indignant displeasure or persistent ill will at something regarded as a wrong, insult, or injury."

Resentment can expand when we focus on broken promises, the insult we feel when the birth parent gets the glory, and the nightmare we live with because the children were hurt. This is self-centered. In a world where people look only at their personal circumstances, we are called as Christians to see like God does. To go beyond ourselves, putting His will before our own.

God put us in a position of authority to nurture these children, provide them safety, and love them. The task is not always joyful. Raising foster children in our society is a challenge. Second Thessalonians 3:13 encourages us to stay firm in doing what is right, "And as for you, brothers and sisters, never tire of doing what is good." We strive to teach foster children how to become productive, well-adjusted adults. The work we do is for a short season of their lives.

When times come and you feel the resentment begin to burn, remember Jesus was persecuted, beaten, and died for you. Set your hearts on what is above not here on earth. He will show you the beauty of what you are doing.

> *God, we pray our resentments would be released so our faith may be used well. Do not allow our feelings to fester, stunting our spiritual growth. Help us to let go and empower us to experience the greater things You have waiting. Let us see as Your see. We give You this day. Amen.*

---

[1] Merriam-Webster, s.v. "resentment (n)," accessed March 16, 2019, http://www.merriam-webster.com/dictionary/resentment

Fostering the Heart Action

Look for feelings of unrest, then pray for a change in perspective. Recognize the gift God has given you and His love for you. Refocus your attention on the situations where you can make a difference and release yourself from what only God can do.

Going Deeper in Scripture: Romans 12:21; Mark 11:25; James 1:19-20

Your Thoughts

_____

_____

_____

_____

_____

_____

_____

_____

_____

_____

_____

_____

_____

_____

_____

_____

_____

_____

25
One More Thing

"Cast your cares on the LORD and he will sustain you;
he will never let the righteous be shaken."

-Psalm 55:22

Large, fluffy snowflakes drifted down. The wind was still as white piles of fluff gathered on tree branches and blanketed the ground. An absolutely beautiful sight.

My shoulders dropped. Sighing, all I saw was more work. *Which do I do first—shovel, or begin the search for the kids' snow pants, mittens, hats, and boots?* All of which translated into more laundry and mopping tracks across the floor, not to mention the extra bumps and bruises from the children's sledding adventures. Slippery roads promised driving complications both at school and work. More burdens in a day packed with things to accomplish.

Do you ever feel like you cannot handle one more thing? Something small like snow can be the complication which takes you over the edge of your remaining strength and sanity. For foster parents, the burden might be something more substantial like a court date you would rather avoid, or another uncomfortable family meeting that goes around in circles, never ending in a decision. Problems can pile up until you cry out to God, *not one more thing. I can't take it.*

But the truth is, you do not have to take it; God does. He will sustain you. Sink into God's strength, peace, and joy. Ask Him to move your feet, mind, and heart forward, one step at a time. The need to turn your struggles over to Him can be felt minute-by-minute at first, then hour-to-hour, then day-to-day as casting your cares on Him becomes more second nature. The good news is God is with you! Release your concerns and fears at His feet.

As foster parents, we can hold onto all that needs to be completed. We can place expectations on ourselves and on the children that are too high.

I would love to have one kid stop wetting the bed. If you look at the issue through the filter of a normal pattern of growth, a child this age should stay dry through the night, but a background of trauma can delay typical development. On days when I am worn out from doing additional loads of laundry, I wonder how much at this point is learned behavior verses abuse related. It leads to frustration when the child needs understanding.

Other days, our compassion and emotions can add stress as we focus on the facts of what the children have gone through. We cannot change the past only the present. If we get tired of dealing with unruly behavior, we can feel guilty because they have it so much worse than we do.

When we struggle, it may be hard to admit, but God knows the intimate details of our lives, and He knows the ending. It is not up to us to change the future. You are free from the burden of thinking everything is about your actions and reactions. God will carry the load. Teaming up with Him means allowing Him to guide our steps, releasing control, and humbly relying on Him to sustain us, so we will not be shaken.

God, we cast our cares on You. We ask You to sustain us through our trials, recognizing You are using them to refine us, so we may become more like You. Help us to get through this day, this moment. We lean into You so we will not lose sight of the greater purpose You have given us. Thank You for not making us do this without You but supporting us with Your great, almighty power. Amen.

Fostering the Heart Action

Take a realistic look at yourself. Whose expectations are you living up to, yours or Gods? Make a list of the things going on in your life. Focus on one task at a time. Decide whether it is imperative that it be done today, or can you finish it tomorrow when there is not as much scheduled? Is it even necessary? As you complete a task, scratch it off the list. It will give you a sense of accomplishment and help you to see an accurate view of what you are doing in your life.

Going Deeper in Scripture: 1 Peter 5:7: Psalm 68:19-20: Matthew 11:28-29

Your Thoughts

_____

_____

_____

_____

_____

_____

_____

_____

_____

_____

_____

_____

_____

26
Sack Lunches

"For he has rescued us from the dominion of darkness and
brought us into the kingdom of the Son he loves, in whom we have
redemption, the forgiveness of sins."
Colossians 1:13-14

For many years I made sack lunches for my four children. I hated doing it. Yet, I did it for them, mostly because I got tired of hearing them complain about school food. Over the years, I became resentful. It was the extra work that put me over the edge of sanity. The time, money, grocery shopping, even the thought process of preplanning and still not doing it "well enough" to satisfy someone. It simply broke me. So, when my kids grew up and left for college, I was grateful to no longer be making sack lunches.

Little did I know I would eventually be blessed with foster kids. Not wanting to begin this new relationship with stress, I protected myself by making a firm decision not to ever make brown bag meals. Eventually, they began asking for them, and I refused. The eldest began to badger me continually. One morning, my temper stretched to its limit, and I started arguing with the eleven-year-old. Slowly, it sank into my brain: I was being ridiculous. Grumpily, I told the child to make it themselves, but only this one time.

By the time we got to breakfast, I recognized I could not ignore my bad behavior. I was a terribly unreasonable example. So, I led the children in prayers, "God, forgive me for losing my patience. I realize for me this was a trigger of frustration and anger. I apologize to You and the kids. Thank You for letting me see and help me to change this in me."

In the end, my wrong actions were redeemed. The kids were able to see an example of humbling yourself before the Lord, asking and receiving forgiveness. God used this to teach not only me, but my foster children how to accept responsibility for personal actions. They were raised with parents who diverted blame for their behavior on to the kids, others, the enemy of our soul, or circumstances. By admitting my fault, asking for forgiveness, and receiving it, I showed them I too make mistakes and need grace.

Foster children are rescued from darkness. They come into our homes so we can show them God's love. Jesus came to this world so we might be forgiven from sin and redeemed to live in Christ forever.

The kids often hold onto blame from their past which is not their own. By being transparent, we show them how to accept our own portion of fault *without* taking on responsibility for issues that aren't ours to own, and how to receive and offer forgiveness. We also establish that God loves us just as we are. Hopefully, it closes the gap between what they perceive themselves to be and what they truly are.

> *Father, thank You for forgiving our sins. We recognize we all have fallen short, but You redeem our mistakes. Use our downfalls to teach us compassion, love, and respect for others. Fill us with Your Holy Spirit so we may shower it over those around us. We pray we will develop into the people You want us to be. We cannot do it without Your touch. Amen.*

Fostering the Heart Action

Next time you lose your patience or react poorly in a situation, do not waste it. Stop, review your actions, admit your portion of fault, and involve the kids so they can learn firsthand what it means to be redeemed and forgiven by God.

Going Deeper in Scripture: 1 Corinthians 1:30; Ephesians 1:7-8; Colossians 1:13-14

Your Thoughts

_____

_____

_____

_____

_____

_____

_____

_____

_____

_____

_____

_____

_____

_____

_____

_____

_____

_____

_____

_____

_____

_____

_____

27
Enjoy the Journey

"I have seen something else under the sun:
The race is not to the swift or the battle to the strong,
nor does food come to the wise
or wealth to the brilliant
or favor to the learned;
but time and chance happen to them all."
-Ecclesiastes 9:11

Two hours and another stop. My husband eased out of the vehicle, his deliberate movements a testament of his slow healing after his motorcycle accident. Traveling is a big part of our lives. In the past, we have travelled abroad for ministry, taken long camping trips, made a quick flight across states for a conference, and taken family beach trips. But this time we knew we needed to stay in Colorado. The pain associated with his injuries even after five months prevented anything adventurous. Since our foster children love water, we decided to include several swimming pools. Making the best of our circumstances, we visited family, a small amusement park, and a hot spring where we hoped the warm waters would provide relief for my husband. Unfortunately, we ended up in urgent care.

In retrospect, I missed traveling and pushed for a "real" vacation. In my human nature, I wanted things back to normal faster than was realistic, which resulted in a setback in my husband's healing process. We can do the same thing in our faith journey. We want God to provide direction, a job, a spouse, healing, or a larger ministry, but He wants us to participate in the journey right here in the present, growing in stages. The terrain of the race isn't even but has hills and valleys that God uses to teach all his children. Death, accidents, and family strife happen in all lives, no matter if we are wealthy, poor, college-educated, high school dropouts, whether we have two parents or none. God uses all situations to show us how to relate to others, to prepare us for major shift changes, and to increase our dependence on Him.

Coming home from vacation, we deviated from our route to see the Great Sand Dunes. It was a few steps from the car to the largest sandbox I have ever seen. The kids laughed and squealed with joy while endlessly rolling down the hill, only to jump to their feet and traipse back up. God gave us unexpected joy during our struggles.

Sometimes the direction we envision for ourselves is not the same as God's desire for us. He may put us on dry sand, away from the water we usually love. With each step our feet sink beneath the sand that pulls us deeper. It takes effort to take the next step. We plod along. Even though it takes more time, it can be wiser to change our path to avoid a sinkhole. Heading up the hill, there are days we slide backwards. But when we make it to the top of the knoll, the view of the rolling hills filled with unique shadows and shapes and topped by a blue sky makes the journey complete. God's vista opens before us, and we see the destination to which He's led us. Do not fight the path God has you on; simply walk with Him and know there is a purpose.

Father let us see the nuanced beauty surrounding us. Remind us there are many unexpected possibilities which we cannot even imagine. Let us rejoice on the path to the hilltop, no matter how many times we slide into a valley. Make our steps sure, so we can look up to see that the vast experiences and dreams You have for us are greater than we can imagine. Amen.

Fostering the Heart Action

Look outside of your normal routine for something unique to share with your foster child. It may be visiting a new place, making a collage of pictures, or cooking together, but stop, take the time, and try to see things differently today. Enjoy the moment.

Going Deeper in Scripture: Matthew 6:25-34; James 1:2-4; 1 Kings 19:3-8

Your Thoughts

_____
_____
_____
_____
_____
_____
_____
_____
_____
_____
_____
_____
_____
_____
_____
_____
_____
_____
_____

God's Blessings

28
The Blessing of Friends

*"A friend loves at all times,
and a brother is born for a time of adversity."*
                                        -Proverbs 17:17

Walking into the school office, the staff greeted her with smiles and thanks for being a foster parent. They proceeded to tell her how one of their foster children had played with a kid on the playground. Nothing unusual for most children, but this child had spent the previous year's recesses with head down, scuffing dirt with the toe of their shoe, so this was a significant difference.

Foster children tend to lack social skills and have dysfunctional relationships. They may struggle with trust, attachment and anxiety which are all key components in building friendships. You may see one child direct the actions of others. Some use an overly loud voice to talk over their peers. Or they may physically hurt another child through pushing or hitting.

Giving children time alone to play helps them find out who they are as individuals. Quiet play allows them peace, boosts the development of their imaginations, and helps them learn to make decisions.

Yet while alone play is positive, kids also have an innate need for friendship, which teaches how to interact with others and eases loneliness. Since foster children may be confused about what constitutes a healthy relationship, we need to guide them. Kids naturally gravitate toward others who are like them developmentally, close in age, and have similar interests and personalities. Foster children are vulnerable. They are attracted to familiar patterns, which may draw them back into destructive behavior. Be aware of their friend choices and nurture healthy relationships.

Non-threatening friends encourage them to new experiences and circumstances, which helps them discover new likes. The development of friendship grows the child's self-esteem as they realize they are likable for who they are. It provides someone to lean on when things are rough, which helps them cope. As they work through the difficulties of friendships, they realize how to solve problems. This influences their future roles as parents, coworkers, and productive citizens.

As tough situations arise, help your foster children learn how to be good friends. True friends want what is best for each other. Teach the child to stand by buddies through rough times, be forgiving when mistakes are made, and caring about what happens to their friends. Friendship is not self-focused but brings empathy and compassion.

Just like foster parents need others' counsel when they do not know how to resolve a situation, so do our foster children. Peers who share a belief in God will mutually encourage each other's faith, which promotes trust. "As iron sharpens iron, so one person sharpens another" (Proverbs 27:17). This means we share knowledge, discernment, and insight with each other.

When you see your foster child make a new friend or reach out to a hurting child, it is a blessing to know your guidance is making a difference.

> *Abba Father, let us be examples of selfless friendship, so we may have the authority to speak into our foster child's life. Thank You for teaching us what it means to love one another. When our hearts break while watching others be unfeeling to our foster children, give us compassion, strength, and wisdom to love them. Remind us of what it was like when we were young and how we overcame difficulties in relationships. Amen.*

Fostering the Heart Action

Find an active playground, swimming pool, or library and spend time there. Encourage your foster child to play with other children. Praise them when they have positive interactions, and if they do not, use the situation to teach them how they could have handled it differently or the importance of knowing when another child's action has nothing to do with who your foster child is.

Going Deeper in Scripture: Ecclesiastes 4:10; Romans 1:11-12; 1 John 4:7; Proverbs 18:24

Your Thoughts

_____
_____
_____
_____
_____
_____
_____
_____
_____
_____
_____
_____
_____
_____

29
The Healing Brain

"Then they cried to the LORD in their trouble,
and he saved them from their distress.
He brought them out of darkness, the utter darkness,
and broke away their chains."

-Psalm 107:13-14

"Do you like your hamburger?" I'd asked a simple question, but my foster child froze, eyes widened, and a blank expression obscured their normally engaged face. I am sure it is where the phrase "the deer in the headlight look" came from. When this child reacts this way, they could not answer a question under any circumstances.

This is one of the many responses we see in foster children who've experienced trauma. There are a couple of different factors why. One is the child's brain reacted in fear.

Threat perception in the brain can produce fight, flight, faint, or freeze reactions. The brain stem controls the flow of messages from the body. The amygdala continually processes sensory information. The hippocampus is the portion of the brain which catalogs short-term memories. When the amygdala is triggered by fear, whether the threat is perceived or real, it alerts the hippocampus, which shuts off the retention of short-term memory and dumps cortisol. Excessive amounts of cortisol attack brain cells found around the orbitofrontal cortex, which is where relational attachment starts.

What does this mean to our foster children? They may not remember abuse, they'll have problems forming relationships, and their behavioral responses will be impacted.

For example, if you smell fresh baked cookies and feel happy, it is because it has triggered a pleasant memory. For children of trauma, if a parent became abusive while drinking alcohol, the aroma may produce fear even when the child is safe. The child will literally feel like the past is happening all over again, now, in the present.

Our foster children have been saved from their distress, but behaviors may linger on sleeplessness, depression, fearfulness, aggression, guilt, potty training difficulties, or being easily distracted. Over time, if not addressed, the stress-induced elevated levels of cortisol can compromise the child's immune system, causing ulcers, stomach aches or headaches, and can make them ill.

The good news is that God created the brain to be amazing, so that when a child is placed in a healthy home, it will begin to repair itself. Be patient, though. The damage can be done over the years or in a single instant, but the healing comes slowly.

There are resources to help you with specific behavior struggles. You can talk to your caseworker. Look up local adoption/foster care organizations—many give free tutorials. A topical search online will give you useful information and suggestions. All children filter and react differently, so some ideas may be best left alone, while other choices fit perfectly with your child's needs and personality.

God gave us life. He gives the wisdom and makes the way for us to become healthy and whole. "For you created my inmost being; you knit me together in my mother's womb. I praise you because I am fearfully and wonderfully made; your works are wonderful; I know that full well" (Psalm 139:13-14). God took small cells, gathered them together so each work in sync with the others to produce a breathing, thinking, amazing child. Foster children have had outside influences which were not of God and caused them pain. The Lord brought them out of the darkness to you because He loves them.

> *Lord, thank you for Your sovereignty over all things. You have*
> *knit us together perfectly. We ask you to reconnect the pieces of*
> *our children's brains so they may overcome. Give us Your wisdom*

*and direction in how to help our foster children. When we are
stressed by the behaviors of our children, remind us that our
brains are affected the same way, so we need to recognize when to
rest and restore ourselves. Help us to know when to reach out to
others for help. Amen.*

Fostering the Heart Action

When you are impatient and want an immediate response to
your request, stop. Instead, take a less forceful approach. Allow extra
time for your foster child to respond. Be supportive and work with
them. Look for alternatives. Watch the child's reactions to smell,
situations, and environments, and then use that data to create
surroundings in which the child will be more likely to feel safe and do
well.

Going Deeper in Scripture: Genesis 2:7; Jeremiah 30:15-17; 3 John
1:2

Your Thoughts

_____

_____

_____

_____

_____

_____

_____

_____

_____

30
Adoption into A Family

*"For he chose us in him before the creation of the world to be holy
and blameless in his sight. In love he predestined us for adoption
to sonship through Jesus Christ, in accordance with his pleasure
and will—to the praise of his glorious grace, which he has freely
given us in the One he loves."*

-Ephesians 1:4-6

My husband's unusual eye shape has been a conversation piece since he was young. Everyone seems to have a theory on why they look exotic. We have no knowledge of his ancestry and do not want to have his DNA tested to find out. Although he is blessed with wonderful adoptive parents, on occasion he has wondered about his birth parents.

Foster children typically know who their parents are, but they struggle with the loss of their families, even when the family dynamics are dysfunctional. They become disconnected and feel abandoned. It is our tenuous task to create a reassuring family life with them, while knowing they could be returned to their birth homes at virtually any time. Not an easy undertaking.

As a foster family, you may have experienced "the look." It is when someone stares at your blended family with a puzzled frown. Or when you run into someone who knows the kids from their previous home. They are trying to figure out why you are with these children. On occasion, some simply ask, "are they yours?" I answer truthfully, "yes."

They are mine, not just for the time they live in my house, but in my heart and prayers forever.

Our family includes seven children. One is my biological child. My husband has three from a previous marriage. The most recent addition is three young foster children. Just as God has adopted us into a family, we have joined our hearts into one, following His example. Our older children loved and embraced the little ones as siblings immediately. This was not a small task—these children were rescued from an abusive home. Their behavior, especially in the early years was tough. The little ones need our time, finances, and attention which used to be directed at our older kids. Only through God's Spirit can we genuinely love and accept new children into our lives.

When God adopted me, He did not say, "that is one of those *problem* kids. I think I will pick the easy one over there." Instead, He said. "Oh, my broken child, come to Me, and I will heal you.' He opened His arms and loved me into His family. Foster, kinship, and adopted children come with faults, dysfunction, and trauma. We need to love them without reservation, just as God, our heavenly Father, loves them.

When it gets tough, turn to God's scripture, the support of others, and sometimes take a respite. Remember, your identity is in Christ and so is theirs. Before long, God will knit your heart and mind together. You can stand firm in the knowledge He will give you the wisdom, perseverance, and unconditional love to do the precious work of parenting.

> *God, grant us serenity to fulfill this high calling. Help us to be the best parents we can be. I pray for more patience, kindness, a gentle spirit, and loving hands to help in Your great work of mending and healing families. May we always lean into Your strength and guidance. Thank You for trusting us. Amen.*

Fostering the Heart Action

Simple activities like eating together can increase connection. Ask each person how their day went. Plan family activities which invite everyone's participation in building unity. Playing board games, taking a walk, visiting friends, or special outings are all ideas you may consider.

Going Deeper in Scripture: 2 Kings 13:23; Romans 8:14-17; 1 John 3:1-2

Your Thoughts

_____

_____

_____

_____

_____

_____

_____

_____

_____

_____

_____

_____

_____

_____

_____

_____

_____

_____

31
Lightening the Load

"Take My yoke upon you and learn from me, for I am gentle and humble in heart, and you will find rest for your souls."
-Matthew 11:29

Today was one of those days. I dropped the soap in the shower. Not a particularly important thing, but an announcement of how my day would go. After cleaning up a broken glass, dealing with quarrelling children, and finding out I had another school fundraiser to participate in, I looked around my messy house. *What am I doing? I chose to bring three little foster children into my home and raise them. God help me, I am crazy!*

I cannot do this. The thought pounded through my brain on repeat. I ask myself why. This arrangement was supposed to last six months, not years. I am too old for this. I raised my children. My time is done.

But God does not release me from loving these special, unique children who did not have a choice in leaving their home, or in having been abused in the first place. The weight lightens though, as God puts on the yoke beside me, like two oxen who shared the load of pulling a wagon through the fields. The Lord whispers encouragement in my ear and nudges my foot forward one step. Before I know it, He and I have plowed one lane down. The broken glass cleaned up, together we turned to mediate the quarrel. Putting aside the fund raiser, we pull through the heavy mess, clearing the path for the planting of new seed.

When you hear a little giggle or a soft-spoken "Mommy," it is reassurance you are doing well. God asked you to partner with Him, not to do it on your own. He does not judge you for the weak days. He listens to your pleas, frustrations, and groanings. He understands disappointments and failure. Yet, He redeems them into new wisdom, patience, and kindness.

It is humbling to know we have been chosen by God to serve Him in the delicate task of raising foster children. This privilege deepens our faith as we see it played out in the details of our days. We learn to trust God in a more intimate way and to feel His mighty power when we are weak. "Jesus looked at them and said, 'With man this is impossible, but with God all things are possible'" (Matthew 19:26).

We can be our own worst obstacles when we dwell on things that we do not have or cannot get. Like time to ourselves or quiet moments. If I focus on a disagreement with a team member who does not believe in my way of dealing with my foster child, then it can fester and control my thoughts. I can become harsh, or prideful to win my point. These are the moments I pray God will transform my heart, spirit, and mind.

The Bible tells us King David flooded his bed with weeping. David said his eyes grew weak with sorrow, and he was surrounded by foes. He cried out to God for mercy, and the Lord accepted his prayer. God will do the same for you. He made David a man after His own heart. Think of the possibilities if we move ourselves out of the way. Imagine what God can do with us. It is unlimited, amazing. Our journey will change the lives around us, as well as our own.

We praise You God and thank You. We recognize You have blessed us richly to even allow us to be able to have extra to share with a child. Help us to be teachable, gentle in spirit, and humble of heart. Ease the path when we falter and lift us into Your restful embrace. Amen.

Fostering the Heart Action

When you are having a difficult day, let it out. Talk to God. Tell Him all your struggles, your hardships, even if they feel selfish. He has large shoulders and can take it. Then after you have spilled your gunky feelings, thank Him for the many blessings you have been given.

Going Deeper in Scripture: Luke 18:27; Matthew 17:20; 1 Samuel 13:14; Psalm 6:6-9

Your Thoughts

_____

_____

_____

_____

_____

_____

_____

_____

_____

_____

_____

_____

_____

_____

_____

_____

_____

_____

_____

_____

32
Life's Moments

*"But now, for a brief moment, the Lord our God has been
gracious in leaving us a remnant and giving us a firm place in his
sanctuary, and so our God gives light to our eyes and a little relief
in our bondage."*

-Ezra 9:8

Life is made up of a series of moments. Some are precious, like
the first time you see your child's face. Others are complicated or
painful. Personally, I despise the second I realize I have unintentionally
sinned.

God calls us to use our time for Him. He asks us to gently love
the world, showering His light upon those around us. Walking
faithfully to His teachings in the Bible.

My husband received a call late one night. He was needed at the
hospital. When he arrived, the family gathered around their loved one
to say good-bye. They held the patient's paper-thin hand one last time.

My husband could not fix what was about to take place, but he
could offer God's love and comfort. He watched as the person's lungs
slowly filled and released one last time. The soul left the shell which
had been a living body. It was an instant of emotional conflict: sadness
for the death but hope in knowing they would see their loved one again
in Heaven.

Moments can be life altering. For example: If a child tells you
how a man touched them improperly or how they were punished. Hold
your breath and pray the child will release the secret binding them. Ask
God for words to encourage and for strength to not push away from

the things you do not want to hear, knowing your listening will help the child heal. God gives us sanctuary with His Spirit. These revelations allow foster children to take one step towards significant change in their lives. Not everyone is in the position to be called to death beds or to hear deep, broken secrets, but as foster parents, we often get more opportunities.

People have the power to impact those around them by offering gentle moments to others. We can open doors, give smiles, encourage each other with words, hugs, and love. When our time comes to leave, do we want our moments to have counted or are we willing to risk having spent them in self-indulgence, indifference, spitefulness, and meaningless trivialities?

I pray I will look back and not see a life of waste, but that I will listen to God's call and do His will throughout the day, every day. This is my prayer for you, too.

Sometimes we are blessed with moments of breathtaking beauty, like watching a child sing or dance, read a difficult passage in a book, or make a friend. These are affirmations that you are doing something right. Embrace these special times for what they are: hope.

Lord, give us the ability to open our hearts. Bring light to our eyes and relief from the sins that bind us in this world. We know You are near, watching over, and preparing a place for us in Heaven. You tell us no person knows when You will return. So, we pray we will see each moment You give us as an expression of Your blessings. Abba Father, thank You for hope. Let us not waste the time You give but allow us to treasure the moments. Amen.

Fostering the Heart Action

Take this moment to stop. Look around, breathe the scent of the air, feel the textures under your fingertips, listen, and taste what is before you. How do you feel? Anxious, excited, peaceful, or confused? What do you see? The beauty of nature, a Bible, a loved one's face? Look at the details. Is the sun warm, are the pages creased, are the eyes crinkled at the edge telling stories of laughter? Appreciate what God is saying to you right now. Step away from sin and allow Him to smooth the path.

Going Deeper in Scripture: 2 Timothy 3:16; Isaiah 43:18-19; James 4:14

Your Thoughts

_____
_____
_____
_____
_____
_____
_____
_____
_____
_____
_____
_____
_____
_____
_____
_____

33
True Act of Worship

"Yet a time is coming and has now come when the true worshipers will worship the Father in the Spirit and in truth, for they are the kind of worshipers the Father seeks. God is spirit, and his worshipers must worship in the Spirit and in truth."

-John 4:23-24

My foster child and I spent a week in Guatemala building homes for displaced volcano victims and teaching of God's love. At one point, we entered a small outdoor enclosure tucked between two buildings. Rough stone and a small tent provided shelter from the warm sun and rain.

Before entering, we were told one man we would meet there had lost 51 family members, and others had scars from the hot lava. I asked my foster child if they could handle what we would see. Not only did my child not flinch, but they embraced the small children whose entire sides were covered in crumpled flesh where burns were still healing. The children were given Bible story coloring sheets. My foster kid helped one girl who pointed to crayons, and then where to color, since she was unable to use what remained of her hands.

During the week, my foster child gave testimony of how they came to live with us. The mission team members were moved to tears as my child described being removed from their home. By the end of the week, it was obvious this child had a servant heart. My foster child reached out to others and touched lives. It helped to heal some of the broken pieces in their life. As we toured, dedicating the houses we built to the Lord and giving them to the families, it was impressed upon me that this was a true act of worship: to unselfishly and generously give for no reason but to show God's love to others.

Foster parenting is the same. We do not do it to receive a reward, but to love children with abandon, helping them to heal, grow, and rebuild. There are many frustrations, trials, and much uncertainty which goes along with foster parenting. God gives us the strength, wisdom, and patience to make it through. When we provide for foster children, we are doing the ultimate act of worship.

Worship is the act of honoring God. No matter where we are, we can show Him our love. Worship is not limited to our presence in a church pew or singing in a choir. Worship is how we live our daily lives by bowing down before the Lord, giving Him all glory and praise. It is knowing there is a God who is greater than we are. In His infinite love, He sent His son to die and be resurrected, so we may have eternal life and relationship with Him.

"Greater love has no one than this: to lay down one's life for one's friends" (John 15:13). We give ourselves for our foster children so they can have happier, healthier lives. The next time you're unable to take time for yourself to do what you want; remember you are fulfilling a high calling for God. Second Corinthians 5:10 tells us, "For we must all appear before the judgment seat of Christ, so that each of us may receive what is due us for the things done while in the body, whether good or bad." There is no escape route; all of us will stand before God. I hope to do it with the shortest list possible. The only way this can happen is to serve the Lord with a pure heart.

Father, we thank You for the blessing of our foster child. May our act of worship be sweet to You. Where we are faltering, uplift us and set us back on a solid foundation. Remind us that our heartfelt actions reflect our honor for You. We pray You will fill us to overflowing with the Holy Spirit so we may bless those around us with all Your grace and mercy. May our lives be a daily worship to You. Amen.

Fostering the Heart Action

Ask God to show you one action to do today that expresses your love for Him as an act of worship. Let it be something only you know about, then give the glory and praise to God.

Going Deeper in Scripture: Psalm 95:1-6; Romans 12:1; Hebrews 12:28-29

Your Thoughts

_____

_____

_____

_____

_____

_____

_____

_____

_____

_____

_____

_____

_____

_____

_____

_____

_____

_____

34

A Positive Difference

"but those who hope in the LORD
will renew their strength.
They will soar on wings like eagles;
they will run and not grow weary,
they will walk and not be faint."

-Isaiah 40:31

Piercing screams carried across the playground. My muscles tensed up. I glanced at my husband—he shared the same look of dread. Slowly we began to rise. At that second, our foster children ran past, laughing. A closer look at the child having a tantrum confirmed it was not, in fact, one of ours. A smile tugged at my lips as I slipped back onto the bench. That was a good day.

The music program was about to begin. Several children in the back of the gymnasium chased each other with shouts of retribution. One knocked over a folding chair with a resounding clunk. Our foster children found good viewing seats and waited for their sibling to perform. When your traumatized kids are better-behaved than the masses, it is a great achievement.

On occasion, all children have pick-on-each-other days. My foster kids were on a roll. After three fights had broken out and I had given them several additional warnings, I was at the end of my patience, so I sent the kids to their rooms. After a half hour, I explained I would soon serve dinner. If they had their rooms picked up, they could come back out but would play by themselves. Not only did they clean their rooms, but one child cleared cluttered dresser tops, while another organized the kids' art supplies and books in the living room. They chose quiet activities to do afterwards, and peace reigned.

I am sharing these moments so foster parents know that what you are doing makes a difference. When traumatized foster kids come into your home, it can be chaotic. Behaviors of control, aggression, staring off into space, undermining each other, nightmares, and all-around craziness can prevail. After you work with these wonderful children and are blessed to see the results, it is worth the hassles. Only God can heal broken children. Let's face it—none of us have enough patience, kindness, graciousness, or love without His generous help. We are blessed to be used as His tools.

Foster parents can achieve amazing results in these resilient children when we dwell on their beauty, as opposed to their bad behavior. Setting a consistent schedule helps the child to know expectations and gives them a sense of security. By establishing a great support team, together we address their mental, physical, and relational needs. On days when you feel like you are doing everything wrong, remember you are making a positive difference—it is simply hard to see in the moment.

1 Thessalonians 5:16-18 tells us to "Rejoice always, pray continually, give thanks in all circumstances; for this is God's will for you in Christ Jesus." When you are discouraged, frustrated, angry, or hurt, ask God to help you to see through His eyes. When we recognize we are a small piece in a large puzzle and know God is in control of years, not just this day, then we can be released from the burden to want to carry things *all* on our shoulders. Put your hope in Christ, and He will renew your strength.

> *Father, thank You for Your lovingkindness. We are so blessed to be used by You to encourage a child to grow to their full potential. Help us to see the minor changes, and then let it be a reminder we are doing a good job. Give us courage to face the things we need to change in ourselves and strength to implement those changes. Help us not to be disheartened but lift us up on wings of eagles. Amen.*

Fostering the Heart Action

Today, watch for the simple changes in your foster child's behavior, then share those observations with your spouse. This will become part of your testimony of faith. Give yourselves a pat on the back and be thankful for the moments of breakthrough.

Going Deeper in Scripture: Galatians 6:9; Jerimiah 24:6; Romans 8:28

Your Thoughts

_____

_____

_____

_____

_____

_____

_____

_____

_____

_____

_____

_____

_____

_____

_____

35
Marriage and Intimacy

*"Therefore shall a man leave his father and his mother, and shall
cleave unto his wife: and they shall be one flesh."*
-Genesis 2:24 (KJV, 1996[2])

Newly married couples show a lot of physical affection. He
offers a hand to help her out of the car, places an arm around her
waist. She hugs him, entwines her fingers through his, or rubs his
shoulders. They linger in a kiss. They each feel loved, special, needed,
and intimate with the other.

Jumping ahead several years, and real life has set in. You both
arrive home tired from work. One of you starts dinner; the other takes
a child to dance class and picks up another from football practice. As
foster parents, you often have the added pressure of counseling
appointments, visits from DHS, GAL, and every other code name you
can imagine.

Hours later, the dishes are clean, the kids' homework is done,
and baths are taken. You glance at the clock. It reads 9:00 p.m. You go
through a mental list of tasks for tomorrow. The news is over, and you
head for bed. On a good day, the evening ends in love making, but
today like so many days, you simply fall asleep exhausted.

If you go too long without kind words, loving gestures, or
intimacy from your spouse, you may start receiving validation from
someone else. It is not intentional. For example, a coworker comments
on how great you did on that presentation. Next you start working

---

[2] Holy Bible: Scofield Study Bible, King James Version. (1996) By Oxford University Press,
United States of America.

together on a project. During that time, you are repeatedly complimented on your creativity. For a person who feels unwanted, unworthy, or unattractive at home, this scenario is like soothing spring rain to parched earth.

Your marriage is your priority under God. If you are not open with each other, the added stress of foster parenting will come between your relationship. When intimacy has disappeared or is in jeopardy, put aside the "he said "she said" tactics and initiate bringing closeness back into your relationship.

The task may be daunting on the surface, but it starts with a small act. Give him a call or text during the day and thank him for working so hard to support the family, or for driving the kids to their appointment. When her hair is in disarray and a child hangs off her hip, remind her she is beautiful. Hold hands as you pray together in the morning. These small intimate acts make us feel wanted, needed, and loved. Remember this is the person who will be with you for your lifetime after the foster child is gone.

It may be awkward at first, especially if it has been a long time. It may require prayer to look past your spouse's blemishes to see something good, but you can. Don't wait for a date night or the right time—start now. Let your spouse know he/she is the person you would marry today.

In Genesis, God said "cleave." This refers to joining oneself with another. We become one flesh spiritually and physically in a lifetime covenant. This is not something to fear, but a union to embrace. If you do not know where to start, read Jesus' teachings. He gives us the greatest example of love.

> *Father, we thank You for the blessings of family and marriage. We ask You to teach us to slow down and remember why we first loved each other. We trust You with the details of our lives, the tasks to be completed. Please free up moments, and place in our hearts the desire to show respect and love to each other. We pray for wisdom on how to express intimacy in our marriage. We ask*

for help to build a solid foundation so that our family will thrive.
Amen.

Fostering the Heart Action

Today, do one thing for your spouse only because you know they will like it. You could stop by work with a cup of their favorite beverage, send flowers for no reason, include a hand-written note in their lunch, text them I love you, or give a massage. Whatever you choose, make sure it is unconditional and without expectations.

Going Deeper in Scripture: Genesis 2:22-24; Proverbs 5:18-19; Malachi 2:16

Your Thoughts

_____

_____

_____

_____

_____

_____

_____

_____

_____

_____

_____

_____

_____

Learning the
Hard Way

36

I Repent

"Yet now I am happy, not because you were made sorry, but because your sorrow led you to repentance. For you became sorrowful as God intended and so were not harmed in any way by us. Godly sorrow brings repentance that leads to salvation and leaves no regret, but worldly sorrow brings death."

-2 Corinthians 7:9-10

Anger twisted his gut, churning into an explosion. The patience he normally prides himself on, gone. An issue he thought they'd moved passed in the last two years had reared its ugly head again: manipulation. The child saw no real problem in lying to someone to get a new item they wanted. How many times did they talk and discipline on this precise subject?

The foster children sat wide eyed and still he fumed. He turned away from them and gripped the counter, breathing hard. Repeating to himself, kids with trauma backgrounds will revert to old patterns if he continues speaking in anger. *He had to back off and not shout.* It pounded against his brain with a rhythm all its own. In that moment, it wasn't their actions which gave him sorrow—it was his own.

He knew he needed to apologize, even though his whole being wanted to hold the grudge so he could justify his behavior. Instead, he prayed for brokenness. He asked God to change his heart, and for the words to speak so the child would recognize he was not excusing their behavior, but not justifying his own either.

It would have been easy for him to regret his anger and hold onto his mistake all day, but it would not help anything. He is an imperfect person. Repenting for his actions, he turned his failure over to God with a sincere heart and asked for change.

If you find yourself in this position, you can try several things. Walk it off until your mind is still enough to pray and listen to God's response. Bite your tongue, not hard, but enough to not retaliate. Spend time reading the Bible. Take a quiet moment in the car and listen to Christian music. Call a friend to pray with you. When your heart is right, ask God for forgiveness and apologize to the children.

We want our foster children to become successful, loving adults. Our imperfection can be a learning ground for them. Be an example by acknowledging your mistakes, requesting forgiveness, and working to change your behavior. It is not enough to say, "I'm sorry." These children have heard that line a hundred times with no truth in it. Whether from their parents or well-intentioned case workers. We need to take the extra step of showing them true repentance and change.

Father, forgive me for not shining Your light, but sometimes reflecting darkness to others. As a Christian, I want to demonstrate the examples You have set for me. I recognize I am incapable of doing this on my own, and I ask You for Your help. Change me from the inside out to become the person You want me to be. I need You, Father, as I need my next breath. On my knees, I make this cry to You. Help me. Amen.

Fostering the Heart Action

Is there something in your life for which you need to ask forgiveness? Repentance opens the heart to allow for change, which makes us closer to Jesus' image. Look around today, and if there is a part of your life, whether a small lie, over-indulging in anything, or something which could be construed as hurtful to your foster child, show them you are willing to change and ask God's help to do it.

Going Deeper in Scripture: Acts 3:18-20; 2 Peter 3:9; Isaiah 61:7

Your Thoughts

_____

_____

_____

_____

_____

_____

_____

_____

_____

_____

_____

_____

_____

_____

_____

_____

_____

_____

_____

_____

_____

_____

_____

37
Work Ethic

"Those who work their land will have abundant food, but those who chase fantasies have no sense."

-Proverbs 12:11

"I need to work late tonight, so you'll be in day care after school," she said. The room filled with groans.

"Do we have to?" a child said.

"Yep," She replied.

"Can't you stay home?" they whined.

They had exhausted the topic of why parents work. Bottom line, to provide for their families. This may not have been the example that was modeled for them in their previous home. How do you instill a work ethic when they have seen parents who work minimally, and when excuses for not going to their job have been the norm?

"I can't get a job because my car's broken." "I'm sick." "The business is too far to drive every day." "Who will watch my kids?" All reasonable considerations, but the problem is that they are continuous excuses. Later it translates into, "I can't make the visit with my kids because…." More of the same justifications.

Work is essential in a family. We can teach responsibility early, by having the children take care of personal belongings. Assigning tasks, even small ones, teaches pride in oneself and spreads out household jobs alleviating the responsibility of all the labor on one person. Tasks can provide a reward when we give our kids allowance or a treat. Children learn self-confidence when they succeed in accomplishing a task, especially when it's something they initially did not think they could do. Satisfaction results when they see the visible outcome.

Opportunity for open communication about the job of cleanliness arose when an unpleasant smell came from one bedroom. Even though we do not have mice in our house, one foster child is fearful of the idea because they previously had them. We talked about personal hygiene and how it affects health. Finding food that remains in their room allowed us to discuss how this attracts mice.

Another child likes to shove everything into hiding places rather than clean their room. It reflects how they dealt with life in their old home: make everything pretty and no one will see the messes hidden in their lives. Going through the child's possessions taught them to get rid of unneeded items, provided easy access to frequently used toys, and increased visibility helped them learn to keep track of things.

Like a messy room, the child can discover how to replace unwanted feelings with positive thoughts and become aware of their behavior.

Foster children may come to you without basic abilities. Even flushing a toilet could be foreign to them. It is important they be taught skills that are new to them without judgment. With my youngest, we played games, hiking dirty clothes like a football, and then the child tossed them into the hamper.

Using the moments of the foster kids' life teaches them the benefits of work. The result is a productive adult life based on confidence in their abilities, strength to not give up when difficulties arise, self-respect, and satisfaction in who they become.

> *Lord, help us to teach our kids how to enjoy work. Let us be positive examples so that they may have an abundant life, facing truth, not living in a fantasy. Let them see Your blessings. We promise to be the first people to believe in their abilities and to encourage them on their path. Amen.*

Fostering the Heart Action

Pick one work-related activity for each foster child. How are they currently doing it (or not completing the task)? Does it reflect a stumbling block from the past? Creatively search for a new way to make it enjoyable. Spend the time together; teach them to see the work in a positive way. If you have limited time and several foster children, pick one a week to work with.

Going Deeper in Scripture: Proverbs 16:3; Proverbs 14:23; Ephesians 4:28

Your Thoughts

_____

_____

_____

_____

_____

_____

_____

_____

_____

_____

_____

_____

_____

38
Steal No Longer

"You shall not steal."

-Exodus 20:15

I imagined incriminating eyes watching my movements. My hand clutched the twenty-five-cent yarn animal stuffed in my front pocket. Creeping through the store aisles, I made it to the front door, bursting into freedom. Or so I thought. I did not get caught pilfering the toy, but guilt grew knowing what I did was wrong. I gave the item away, asking God for forgiveness, but at no time admitting my shame aloud. I would never steal again.

When foster children entered our life, they were in an emergency placement, so we never experienced the required foster parent courses. As a precaution, I put away medications and money. Generally, I prefer to trust first, but no one needs temptation.

God views all acts of stealing equally; a sin is no larger or smaller because of how culture perceives it. It could be pilfering a pack of gum from a family member's purse, taking a friend's sunglasses without permission, or ripping off a shirt from a store. These actions can multiply if left unattended. The long-term health and happiness of a child is at stake.

When one child started stealing belongings from another, we implemented some safeguards. We began using piggy banks to hold money and added rules about not being in someone's room unless invited. If we teach them in our home not to take someone else's things, it is easier to translate that ethic to friend's home, store, or school. Ask the child how they would feel or react if someone stole from them, then apply it to the child they took the item from. This encourages empathy. Talk about what kind of friend they want to both be and have.

Foster children may steal for several reasons. Abused children can feel they are entitled to the item even without paying because no one cares. It can be a self-soothing technique when someone has hurt them. When foster kids see their future as hopeless, stealing is a way to gain attention. If they feel inconsequential, the kids believe their actions do not matter. Theft can be a way they gain control over their crazy lives. In some cases, it is taught by their birth parents.

We do a disservice when we let foster kids slide because we feel sorry for the way they were brought up. They cannot stay victims but need to learn consequences. Have them apologize verbally or in writing to the person who they stole from. Ground them from activities or possessions and have them earn the privileges back. Give time outs when appropriate. Incorporate proactive strategies to eliminant temptation before it becomes a problem. When these children become adults, it's too late to change their behaviors. Stealing will lead to jail time.

I noticed my littlest chewing gum we did not provide. After careful questioning, they confessed to taking the item from the grocery store. After a time out, we went to the store. The child apologized and paid for the pillaged item. When I took the yarn toy, I immediately felt convicted inside. With this child, we needed to teach them the consequences.

Problems of stealing will diminish over time with repeated, appropriate consequences, and as children heal. Be aware of what is going on around you. Ask the children questions if items you don't recognize appear in your home. When you discipline, remind the foster child God calls us to gain knowledge from our mistakes and move on. Our errors do not define who we are. We still love them.

Father God, help us to be vigilant. When we see stealing, let us be able to teach remorse, empathy, and consequences. Give us strength to be stern but continue to love the children in our care.

Where uncaring, false ways have been taught in their past, give us direction to show them a positive way to live. Amen.

Fostering the Heart Action

When you catch a child stealing, take a deep breath. Recognize their actions are not a reflection on you. Discipline out of love. Read about this topic to the child either in the Bible or a children's book. Help them to understand how stealing affects others and the consequences if they continue in the behavior.

Going Deeper in Scripture: Ephesians 4:28; John 10:10; James 1:13

Your Thoughts

_____

_____

_____

_____

_____

_____

_____

_____

_____

_____

_____

_____

_____

_____

39
Looking Beyond Food

"Dear friend, I pray that you may enjoy good health and that all may go well with you, even as your soul is getting along well."
-3 John 1:2

Picking up the clothes strewn across the floor, she unearthed food wrappers. On further investigation, she found a stash of crackers and a lot of empty bags of chips. This is not a one-time incident. It can be very inconvenient when you go to pull out an item to fix dinner and it is gone, devoured by your foster kid.

Hording food can be a survival mechanism. Some of these kids previously did not know when they would next be fed. The older kids learned to feed the smaller ones, with whatever they could find. This becomes a control issue of what and when they eat. Stealth trips to raid the pantry are a symptom of a deeper problem.

Once foster children come into our homes, food manipulation can be the first behavior that arises, which clearly indicates neglect. On our foster children's intake sheet, it said they were healthy eaters. We did not understand what this meant was they liked junk food twenty-four/seven.

When I prepared a healthy, balanced meal, their eyes opened wide, and their jaws dropped. One of the kids tentatively picked up a fork and pushed it around the plate. I learned to slowly integrate foods they were used to with healthier choices. Unfortunately, I gained weight in the process.

It became apparent we had to put less food on their plates because they always asked for seconds. The amount of food was not the issue; it was having more. For some kids, it is a survival skill. They learned to eat when food was available because it was not always there. Binge eating can be an issue as well. Left unchecked, these children can eat adult size portions. Competitive eating is when one child asks for food and the others follow their lead even when not hungry. They watch you, so start with your eating habits. Eat only at mealtimes.

To combat food issues, we must teach healthy habits, and provide them security. Establish a routine of three nutritional meals and two snacks a day. They will be reassured food is coming and there is plenty. None of us want to be stuck in the kitchen all day prepping food. Plan for simple snacks. Give them two healthy choices to pick from or leave a bowl out which they can pull from once a day when they want. For school days, pack the items in their bags. It will give them control so they can focus on school.

Teach them how to balance their choices. They can have chips or dessert but not at every meal. Do not try to put them on a diet or use food as a reward. Instead, advocate an all-around fit lifestyle including healthy food, exercise, mental breaks, play, and tasks.

At mealtime do not make them eat everything on their plates but do let them know this is the food being served. If they do not finish, keep the plate handy in case they get hungry later. The kids will not starve if they choose not to eat.

Teach good routines of cleaning up after oneself, they learn responsibility and what it is like to be part of a family. Each child should help set, clear, and wash dishes.

The bottom line is, the kids use food to comfort, control, and try to fix their mixed-up lives. As they get settled and feel more secure, their souls will start to heal, and this problem will lessen. It will take a lifetime; behaviors cannot be changed overnight.

> *Father, we pray we will be instruments to teach healthy living to the children in our care. Give us words to speak so they will understand. Help us to recognize when we become an obstacle to their healthy eating and redirect our steps to try new methods to*

help the children adjust. You have called us to take care of our bodies for Your service; remind us to be good examples. Amen.

Fostering the Heart Action

Have a child cook with you periodically. Let them help you pick out the menu. Explain how to balance the meal to include nutritious foods. Teach how food provides energy, builds strong bones, and helps our brains to develop. Apply the benefits of healthy food to an activity they enjoy doing. For example, if they like bicycling, tell them how protein improves muscle, helps your immune system, and allows better recovery after pedaling hard.

Going Deeper in Scripture: Haggai 1:5-7; Proverbs 23:1-3; Matthew 6:25-27

Your Thoughts

_____

_____

_____

_____

_____

_____

_____

_____

_____

_____

_____

40
Inner Beauty

"Your beauty should not come from outward adornment, such as elaborate hairstyles and the wearing of gold jewelry or fine clothes. Rather, it should be that of your inner self, the unfading beauty of a gentle and quiet spirit, which is of great worth in God's sight."
-1 Peter 3:3-4

Her black leggings wrapped around her curves, emphasizing her form. The crop top gave glimpses of a flat stomach, smooth, not yet affected by time. Long dark hair flowed in glistening trails down her back. Young men would notice. What they would not have seen was the inner turmoil of her life. The desperation to be seen, cared for, and not abandoned.

Would they see the pain in the teen's eyes, or would they want to take more of her self-worth?

My foster child only saw that this girl was receiving attention and the appearance of being accepted by their peers. It was contrary to our teaching of discretely covering our bodies, or of kindness and healthy love being the most important attributes we can have. Society teaches instant gratification. We have the challenge of showing kids there are more important values, values we achieve by perseverance, overcoming difficulties, and building character.

There are things we can change and other things we cannot. We need to teach our foster daughters and sons they are important, worthy of respect and dignity. God calls us to display ourselves with the unfading beauty of inner worth. He loves us with all our dents, battle scars, and bruises. He sees what we will become.

One of the most difficult tasks given to a foster parent is helping a child realize their inner beauty. In this world where exterior looks open doors, fashion determines acceptance, and conformity to the current political viewpoints prevails, we need to teach children it is okay to be different. Our value comes not from this world, but from the Lord. He calls us to be gentle and quiet in spirit, self-controlled, compassionate, faithful, kind, and to show love even to our enemies. In our own strength we cannot fulfill what God asks, but with His Holy Spirit residing in us as Christ-followers, He gives us the power.

Everyone has had a moment where they felt worthless, belittled, or embarrassed. It may have been when another child laughed when we tripped, we got an answer wrong in front of the whole class, or we failed to make the sports team we desired. These are paltry examples when you add having been sexually assaulted, humiliated by a drunken family member, or told out loud that you're worthless and always will be. Take a moment and try to see through your foster child's eyes.

Where do we begin? Simply by loving the child. Encouraging them, not only with words but with actions, to see the good things in themselves. If they are a good swimmer or just love it, get them into classes. If they're great at reading, get more books and have them read to you. Do they like to draw? Make sure they have plenty of paper and pencils for refrigerator sketches. If they enjoy helping others, include them when serving at local nursing homes, giving out dinners to homeless, or making cookies for neighborhood kids. They may not yet be able to articulate what they enjoy or are good at. You will need to look for their potential greatness, then give them opportunities.

Abba Father, thank You for giving us these precious souls. Your workmanship is perfect, and we want to be used to bring out the best in our foster children. We do not desire to put false promises in their heads, so let us see through Your eyes the infinite potential of what they can become. We want to be true examples to them. Let our failings, successes, and hopes be evident to our foster children, so they see how to live well for You. Amen.

Fostering the Heart Action

Praise your foster child for one thing today that highlights their inner beauty.

Going Deeper in Scripture: Proverbs 3:15-18; Psalm 139:14; 1 Samuel 16:7

Your Thoughts

_____

_____

_____

_____

_____

_____

_____

_____

_____

_____

_____

_____

_____

_____

_____

_____

41

A Spirit of Gentleness

"But the fruit of the Spirit is love, joy, peace, forbearance,
kindness, goodness, faithfulness, gentleness, and self-control."
-Galatians 5:22-23

My foster child woke up grumpy. I could already see it would be a struggle to get them to school on time. Knowing that if I tried to push the kid to speed up, they would get stubborn and slow down, I took a different approach. I held out my hand and said, "Come here, sweetie." Taking a brush, I gently slid it through their hair with even, slow strokes, all the time speaking encouraging and kind words about the day ahead. By the time we were done, this three-minute activity had changed the child's attitude to a cooperative one. They were able to get ready for the day in a timely manner.

Although I strive to be consistently kind in my approach to others, some days I cannot find a drop of kindness within me. It is easy to be gentle with a child who is physically hurt or crying, but when they are cranky and in need of a nap, not so much. Especially when it is a pattern. I sometimes allow my frustration to flow outward, plowing through life like an elephant trampling vegetation under its feet. Only it is an already broken child who gets trampled. It is in such moments that I hear God's whisper: slow down; be easy. I have given you a life rich in love and you can show it to this child.

When the little tug God sends me does not change my attitude, I take a deep breath and walk away, giving myself permission for a time out. I recognize that in my own strength, I have no good, kind, gentle words to speak. After fifteen minutes of prayer, I am composed enough to share God's love and truth with the child, allowing us to have a great, honest conversation. On occasion, I must apologize for saying something in an unkind way, bringing death with my words instead of life.

On busy days, when I cannot sequester myself, I am reminded of the adage, "If you can't say anything nice, don't say anything at all." I clamp my lips together and pray silently for God to get me through. I desire to be a good example for them. These children saw enough rollercoaster emotions and behaviors in their previous life.

When we correct them kindly, they are more likely to change their actions. They will respond less harshly, and old coping mechanisms will be less likely to arise. It is important to teach them positive ways to deal with their emotions, including giving them permission to step away for a moment which is a lifelong strategy for getting their reactions in check.

Sometimes, remembering where the children came from evokes enough empathy we can soften our approach. God calls us to have a spirit of gentleness, yet He does not expect us to do this on our own. He gives us the ability to think through our responses and adjust them to fit His desire for us, which is that we be a living example of Him.

> *Father, we pray for Your spirit of gentleness. Please help us to recognize our own sin and remove it. When times are trying, we pray for Your redirection and wisdom to try new approaches. We know it is not within ourselves, but a gift You give us. We humbly ask You to fill us with Your Holy Spirit, so that we may be used as a tool to help others. We pray for these things in Your Holy name. Amen.*

Fostering the Heart Action

Practice being gentle in manner during the least stressful times. When your schedule allows, plan calm, compassionate tasks to do with your foster child. Art projects, reading books, even the rhythmic throw of a baseball will help the two of you bond and build a better relationship. Over time, gentleness will become second nature to you, and your foster child will learn the benefit of quiet play.

Going Deeper in Scripture: Galatians 6:1; 2 Timothy 2:25; Philippians 4:5

Your Thoughts

_____

_____

_____

_____

_____

_____

_____

_____

_____

_____

_____

_____

_____

_____

_____

_____

_____

_____

_____

_____

_____

42

Fear Traps

"So do not fear, for I am with you;
do not be dismayed, for I am your God.
I will strengthen you and help you;
I will uphold you with my righteous right hand."

-Isaiah 41:10

We all have fears. Mine are mice. Growing up, we lived near a corn field, so from time to time I had an unwanted visitor scurrying through my bedroom. The small creature could not hurt me, but for whatever reason—reasonable or not—I was scared.

Our foster children have fears we may never understand. They run in terror from flies, but allow roly-poly bugs to crawl all over them, which, in my opinion, is more disgusting. The terror evoked by a tiny fly has no apparent rhyme or reason that I can see. It is simply a fact.

When foster children first arrive, nightmares may be continuous. You should expect your bedroom door to revolve as they need you. You may find a child sleeping on the couch closest to your bedroom. Or a child who reacts unusually to water or a mirror. Foster children's reactions to fears are different for all kids, so adjust and look for the hidden meaning.

Foster parents guide the children through these moments when they are afraid. I admit as I hear piercing screams yet again, or a lamp tumble to the ground in the scamper away from a fly, it can be hard to be patient, loving, and kind. But that is exactly what God calls us to be. It's important to acknowledge their distress but teach them not to allow it to control them. They have enough real nightmares to deal with to allow simple life to cause unnecessary ones.

In our society, we like to name everything from a fear of spiders to ADHD, or anxiety. We have a name it and claim it approach. Foster children are not the sum of their dysfunction. Teaching them they are stronger than a name is very important.

In our home, it was a nightly routine to reassure one child the doors and windows were locked and secure. No one would get them. They were safe. We were battling real anxiety. While terror can be based on truth, at other times the fear is simply perceived. When a child in our care begins to see shadows morph into monsters, we need to reassure and teach how our brains can make us believe something untrue when we concentrate on it. Putting focus on happy thoughts or reading a joy filled book at bedtime can help them sleep. Leave nightmare discussions for the morning.

To alleviate fright, let them know you are available at any time, particularly at night. Plan out the best way to do this. It can be yelling out, ringing a bell, or inviting them to come get you.

The first night one of our kids had a nightmare *un*related to their past, I wanted to dance with excitement. *This was normal!* It was hard to contain my emotion of relief as I sympathized with them. These beautiful, precious children have been placed into our care by God to cherish and direct towards healing.

Talk about the difference between real fear and what is merely imagined. Our inner voices are used by God to protect us from making costly mistakes. Pray with your children for protection and to be enveloped in God's love. Help them to express their feelings and consider why they might have them. Some will be easy to explain, while others will never be understood. Make sure they know it is alright not to know everything.

> *God, we pray You will give us understanding, grace, and love even when we feel far from it. Give our foster children comfort, freeing them from the trap of fear. Give us wisdom to show them how to admit and overcome distress. Reveal any history we need to know*

so we can help them be released from past nightmares, but do not let our minds dwell there. You are the great Healer, and we ask You to be that for these beautiful children. Amen.

Fostering the Heart Action

This week talk to your foster child about what scares them. When learning to confront that fear, break it down into small pieces so it is not overwhelming. For a child afraid of the dark, a night light helps, but reading together with a flashlight does too. Explain some of your anxieties and tell them how you deal with them. Reassure them they will always be safe with you.

Going Deeper in Scripture: Psalm 23:1-6; 1 John 4:18; 2 Timothy 1:7

Your Thoughts

_____

_____

_____

_____

_____

_____

_____

_____

_____

_____

_____

_____

_____

Releasing the Captives: Freedom from the Past

43
Coping with Sexual Abuse

"I will instruct you and teach you in the way you should go;
I will counsel you with my loving eye on you."

-Psalm 32:8

Sexual situations are not simple and can be extremely uncomfortable. God gave us sexual desire to express in a loving intimate relationship. Foster children will have these desires, but if they experienced molestation or voyeurism, they may become confused about what those feelings mean.

We should create a safe environment with open and honest communication. Children all react differently to their abuse. The child may feel guilty because they derived pleasure from the inappropriate touch. They may miss the abuser, often a family member. The child can be embarrassed, angry, take the blame for not saying no, or believe they caused the action. For some raised from birth with sexual abuse it becomes a normal way to receive attention.

Foster children need to be told abuse is not their fault. The perpetrator led them through experiences they should never have had. Abusers may use physical force, but they can also groom them into it using play, deception, threats, or other forms of pressure to get the child to participate and keep silent. The lines between healthy and harmful behaviors become blurred, so foster parents can help kids work through individual emotions.

Children of sexual abuse may have sensory processing issues, withdraw into themselves, lack empathy towards others or animals, or have anger and aggression issues. They are at risk of becoming perpetrators. Educate yourself to effectively encourage healing. If you have multiple kids, even from the same family, individualize their recovery plans for their personalities.

Set up clear guidelines for your home. Since foster children's personal space and boundaries have been violated, teach them appropriate limits. Help them to discern between a good hug and when it is intrusive to others. Intervene when they talk over each other or try to control each other's behaviors. Remind them to listen to and respect one another's voices and needs.

Sexual exploration happens even in non-sexualized kids. We need to distinguish between inappropriate and normal expressions. When getting dressed or showering, establish alone time, close the door, and pull curtains. Reinforce this should occur in their private space. Discuss why—don't ignore them.

Make sure your house is transparent. Add safeguards where necessary. If you know there is a history of sexual abuse, give children separate bedrooms. Nanny cameras outside of bedroom doors might be necessary if a child feels threatened or you see inappropriate behavior.

Children should play with the door open and you within listening distance. Be attentive. If one child is dominant over the others during play, step in and suggest they share leadership while considering their playmates' feelings. If you feel any child is being sexually aggressive, do not leave them alone. The child needs to understand that although they are not responsible for others' actions, they are responsible for their own, and consequences will take place any time they endanger another.

Set up a loving, trusted team to create a vision for healing, but ultimately you must stand up for the best decisions for restoration. Ask God to instruct you in the way you should go.

Father, let us be wise beyond our knowledge. We pray you intervene in sexually abused children's lives. Help them heal. Give us guidance and strength to show these kids Your true love.

One of selflessness. When we work with other professionals, we pray for respect and unity in decisions. Amen.

Fostering the Heart Action

Counseling is good. Make sure you advocate for a counselor that fits the unique situation of the child's needs. Is your current counselor effective? If not, ask to change or explore additional options. When laying a foundation for a child's life, the cost should not control your decisions. Ask a church to help—many have benevolence funds for helping people through challenging times.

Going Deeper in Scripture: Psalm 72:4; Jeremiah 33:6; 1 King 22:5

Your Thoughts

_____

_____

_____

_____

_____

_____

_____

_____

_____

_____

_____

_____

_____

44
Lies Break Trust

"The LORD detests lying lips,
but he delights in people who are trustworthy."
-Proverbs 12:22

The promise was made, "I will see you on Sunday." The lie slipped easily from their lips.

Sunday came and went with no parents in sight. Once again, the foster child was hurt and disappointed.

People lie for many reasons. It could be in imitation of family or friends. Sometimes, they do it for attention or to get what they desire. Other times, it is to avoid punishment or stressful situations. When a child is taught to hide abuse or neglect in the home, things become more complicated. They see nothing wrong with deception. It is like taking an advanced course in prefabrication from the person who is supposed to be your role model instead of the expert in bad character. Habits formed from birth are hard to break.

When I was a child, I was told the story of *The Boy Who Cried Wolf* from *Aesop's Fables.* In the story a boy calls the villagers to rescue him from wolves several times, and each time the villagers arrive to find none. In the end, when a real wolf attacked no one believes his cries, so no one comes to help, and the boy is eaten. The story terrified me. I learned not to lie.

It is not as simple breaking established patterns. Especially in a world where people do not see anything wrong with a "little white lie." Have you ever heard someone say, "Well it doesn't hurt anyone." We know the difference and so does our foster child. They lived a lie.

As adults we have learned not to lie, our actions and words should be the example to our foster children. Not lying allows trust to grow, which gives us a voice into our foster children's lives.

God says nothing is hidden—He knows everything. When one lie builds on another, we can all lose sight of the truth, even the child. Contrast the results of lying with what it looks like to be honest and the privileges we receive by being so. We can encourage the child to tell the truth by not responding harshly when they are forthcoming, but to implement proportional consequences without shaming them.

It's normal to feel frustrated, hurt, angry, or disappointed when your foster child blatantly tells you a lie. And that is okay, but when we decide how to deal with the situation take time for those initial emotions to subside. For minor offenses, you might simply state the fact you know, and then ask the child if they want to stick with their story. If there are life-threatening or legal consequences, you need to explain those and why. Encourage them to make the right decision, but if they cannot, you must step in. There is no easy answer to this problem. It will take time.

When you are overwhelmed, step back and pray. You are only one person and a small piece to the bigger solution. God sees the foster child's heart and will continue to work with them for a lifetime, refining them into trustworthy individuals.

Abba Father, we need Your abundant grace and mercy. We do not always react as we should or understand why our foster children behave in a certain way. Take away the frustration, hurt, and pain from our hearts. Help us to see through Your eyes and let us love as You do. Forgive us and our foster children. Show us how to be trustworthy and allow us a new beginning. Amen.

Fostering the Heart Action

Pay attention to what your foster child is saying. Lying can be a symptom of another problem. What is the situation? Are they trying to divert your attention? What do they have to gain? Give them an opportunity to change their story to the truth. If they chose to stay firm in their deception, present your facts and give them a consequence. Time outs, reading a short book on lying, or writing a paper on what the child gains from being truthful can reinforce what you are sharing.

Going Deeper in Scripture: Colossians 3:9-10; Luke 8:17; Proverbs 21:6

Your Thoughts

_____

_____

_____

_____

_____

_____

_____

_____

_____

_____

_____

_____

_____

_____

_____

_____

_____

45

The Ability to Parent

"Start children off on the way they should go,
and even when they are old they will not turn from it." –

-Proverbs 22:6

The foster children bounded up the stairs. "We're home!"

"How was your visit?"

"Great," they replied, heading off to change into pajamas in preparation for the planned hour of down time before bed. This is the pattern which developed over time to limit behavioral backlash. Later the kids will tell them about the visit, which might have included sleeping all day, talking on the phone to family members who have active no contact orders, or playing unattended in the housing parking lot for hours.

With a sigh, they accepted the basic need for the kids to see their parents, but they wish the parents would spend quality time interacting and watching over the children's safety.

Don't we all feel like that sometimes? Everyone has their own style of raising children. Some have no boundaries, allowing their children to run unattended. Others are overprotective, and don't allow their kids to experience natural consequences or explore their surroundings.

The Bible gives us instructions on how to raise children. Psalm 127:3 tells us children are a reward, a blessing. Proverbs 19:18 instructs us to discipline our kids. Ephesians 6:4 reminds us not to put undue pressure on our kids or unnecessarily frustrate them, but to train them up in the Lord's ways. While we pray parents will have a balanced approach in upbringing, it does not always work that way. Foster parents may see birth parents who neglect, abuse, or put kids at risk. So, it can be difficult.

We want the absolute best for our foster children. Working with the birth parent, we can encourage good parenting skills, set boundaries, pray with them, and be a good example of how-to parent. In these ways, we contribute to helping them learn and grow. Often the parent is required to take a class, but the training provided is limited to basics and realistically there is not much oversite of any practical application of what's taught. Two hours of supervised visits is not comparable to days of living in one home.

When the kids expound on how great their biological parents were during the short visit, we can feel unappreciated. They readily give recognition and love to their parents, but you get all the grief. It can be very discouraging. In truth, they do not understand, but you are their safety. When they reach adulthood, they are more likely to value you. When you need to express your feelings, do so to another trusted adult. Guard your tongue when around the kids. We must be careful not to put them in a position where their hearts and loyalties are torn between their foster and birth families. It's not a competition. Children can love you all.

As a parent, teaching God's love is our number one priority. Salvation will stay with them for a lifetime. Biblical principles will give them practical ways to deal with any situation. Knowing God's love and having an intimate relationship with Him will allow the kids to never feel alone. Faith leads to hope. The children will grow up healthier and happier, and after they leave us, the knowledge of Jesus will go with them.

Abba Father, we pray You will guide our lives, provide knowledge we can impart to our children, and give us a gentle spirit so we can be the type of parents You call us to be. Help us navigate the path of working with biological parents. We want to be a positive influence on their lives, but we cannot do that without You being closely involved in the details. Amen.

Fostering the Heart Action

In our role as foster parents, we make an impact when it's within our power to do so and learn to let go of the things we cannot control. Taking the children to church, reading Bible stories, or singing hymns encourages them to lean into the Lord's strength.

Going Deeper in Scripture: Deuteronomy 6:5-9; Matthew 19:13-15; Colossians 3:21

Your Thoughts

_____

_____

_____

_____

_____

_____

_____

_____

_____

_____

_____

_____

_____

_____

_____

_____

_____

46
God Never Leaves

"The Lord himself goes before you and will be with you; he will never leave you nor forsake you. Do not be afraid; do not be discouraged."

-Deuteronomy 31:8

Children in abusive/neglectful homes learn that they cannot trust. Broken promises and the unpredictability of their lives lead them up and down an uncertain path. As they grow, they discover that if they do not let anyone in, they will not be hurt. They can only rely on themselves. No one else really cares beyond a few months—or moments.

The system reinforces this perspective as social workers change, advocates leave for the next broken child, and courts modify visits or remove a counselor because one of the ten people overseeing the case does not believe the current situation is working.

Considering all this unpredictability and broken trust, the idea that God cares about them can be perceived as ludicrous. The children hold onto anything that is tangible, whether it is healthy or not.

In the time children are with us as foster parents, we can show them we are true to our word, helpful, and loving. We work to get the kids mentally healthy so they can go back to their homes, and then we are gone. Once again reinforcing the idea that no one ever cares forever; the kids must protect themselves.

As adults we understand that the people involved in foster care are stretched thin and realistically only have time to slap a healing bandage over a wound before they need to help the next kid who is in trouble. Like a doctor doing triage in a war zone, it is not their fault. They love the kids; there are just too many children under attack.

So, in our months or years of providing a home for these children, how do we teach them they are never alone? Start with yourself. Do you believe it? Have you seen over your years of experience, even during the troubled times, that God was with you?

When we pray to Him, He listens. When we listen, He speaks to us through the Bible, music, or friends. In the middle of the night, He whispers. If we ask, He wraps His arms around us, letting us know we are never alone. On days we are strong, He trusts us with more to give. We see His faithfulness and recognize when He is moving because of our history with Him. God has used our past to draw us closer to Him and to prepare us to become a foster parent.

Once you recognize that God has been in your life since day one, you can help your foster children to see Him in theirs. When you see Him working, point it out to your kids. Let them experience it with you. Pray with your foster children, then when you recognize God has answered a prayer, talk about it.

God sent these children to us because He knows we can love them, be their advocates, and protect them. He chose us long ago to prepare us to take in kids with trauma backgrounds. Recognizing where we can make a difference and letting go of where we cannot change circumstances will help us and the children to not be discouraged or afraid.

What is in the heart of a foster child can never be taken. It is who they are. God will never leave or forget them. When life happens, they can look up, see the vastness of the sky, know there is something greater than what is immediately happening, and be assured God is watching over them. He will get them through, and someday use what they have learned to help someone else.

Father, we lift the children up to You, laying them at Your feet. We pray You will let Your Holy Spirit surround them, so they never feel alone. Help us to teach them the importance of Your

*love which is greater than the world they live in. And give them
hope for a future not yet realized. Amen.*

Fostering the Heart Action

Lead the children in prayer. Let them see that God is tangible to talk to and He cares about them.

Going Deeper in Scripture: Joshua 24:23; Psalm 28:6-7;
Lamentations 3:31-33

Your Thoughts

_____

_____

_____

_____

_____

_____

_____

_____

_____

_____

_____

_____

_____

_____

_____

_____

47

Forgiving the Unforgivable

"Get rid of all bitterness, rage and anger, brawling and slander, along with every form of malice. Be kind and compassionate to one another, forgiving each other, just as in Christ God forgave you."

-Ephesians 4:31-32

Anger rolled through my body, my mind exploding with thoughts of hate. *How could they do this to us?* It was inexcusable.

I held the grudge, hurt, and pain close to my heart. A daily reminder of what this person's actions did to me. It became a refining time in my life when God taught me a lot about forgiveness. It took months, but eventually with God's help I was released from the bitterness and rage.

Looking into the small faces before me now, I wondered how to teach them forgiveness, but simultaneously keep them safe? If their wounds were allowed to fester, they would live in their trauma and never be set free to move forward.

Forgiveness does not make excuses for the perpetrator, forget it ever happened, or deny the child's feelings. Rather, it is an intentional act of letting go. It changes the kids' perspective toward life and those around them.

Matthew 18:21-22 says we should forgive seventy-seven times those who sin against us. Keeping a list of the hurt separates us from relationship with others. Stuck in the past, we cannot move forward into a healthier life.

When we ask God into our hearts, we initially ask for mercy for our sins. He instantly gives it. As we mature in our relationship with God, we still make mistakes, so we rely on God's understanding to continually forgive.

Teaching foster children to let go of the hold previous abuse has on them does *not* mean allowing them to return to an unsafe environment. Hurtful conduct can never be justified or excused. If a person is truly sorry for what they did, their actions will reflect it. No one can cause them to transform. It is within themselves. Foster children are only responsible for their own behavior—no one else's.

The person who hurt me and my family was not able to see they did anything wrong, so they were not going to change their behavior. I forgave them by looking into their past experiences and seeing through their eyes. Breaking the bitterness which encrusted my heart. This took continual prayer for a few months. Even with forgiveness, putting reasonable boundaries in place is healthy and good. In the end, God freed me from the pain which controlled my thoughts. Helping a foster child to understand is one step toward building a foster child's new life.

> *God, give us the ability to forgive as You have forgiven us. Let us not hold grudges but release us from painful circumstances. Show us how to forgive and keep safe boundaries so we do not continue to be hurt. Thank You for all the examples You show us throughout the Bible. We love you. Amen.*

Fostering the Heart Action

Model what it means to be compassionate. When the children sincerely ask for forgiveness, give it. Be mindful and watch for the behavior to reappear. If they make the same mistake again, tell the child you can forgive them, but you expect to see real change in their lives. This is a promise they are making you. Then give them consequences for any broken promises.

Going Deeper in Scripture: Colossians 3:13; Luke 17:3-4; 1 John 1:9

Your Thoughts

_____

_____

_____

_____

_____

_____

_____

_____

_____

_____

_____

_____

_____

_____

_____

_____

_____

_____

_____

_____

_____

48
Image in Christ

"So God created man in his own image, in the image of God he created him; male and female he created them."

-Genesis 1: 27

I have always had long, brown, curly hair. While I was growing up, society's prevalent hairstyle preference was long, blonde, and straight, which left me often feeling less than pretty.

One morning, my foster child wanted their hair straightened. The child has reached the age where, in their mind, acceptance is dependent on looks. My husband and I both had the same response: "You know, your hair is already straight."

My foster child is beautiful with a creamy complexion and pretty eyes, but that is not what they see. As I watch this child try to balance between our house rules, and what the kids at school promote, I recognize the need to encourage self-esteem and individualism.

Hiding who they are is a survival mechanism to fit in when they feel unsettled. Teach foster children it does not matter what all the other kids do, but what *we* do. Showing our foster children how to respect, care for, and be kind to others even when they are different is invaluable. We should embrace all the many characteristics God has given us and not conform to one way. God made us all unique.

Our identity comes only from Christ, who has created us in His own image. He adopted us as his own, giving us life, and making us into beloved daughters or sons. He loves us as we are, not as we should be. If we want people to accept us, then we must first accept ourselves.

When we ask Christ into our lives, we recognize we are sinners, ask forgiveness, and give leadership of our lives to God. From that point on, He will never leave us, even when we make mistakes. He leads us into all we will be. As we study the Bible and become closer to Christ, we discover more about our own identity.

Being adopted as God's children brings responsibility. He asks us to be the first to show love. We should look beyond obvious behaviors to what hides beneath, then we can teach our foster children compassion, and how to make good decisions.

For instance, there are times when my foster child intentionally aggravates a situation to provoke a negative response. Now, I have a choice to get frustrated or angry. Instead, God shows me that the child is falling back on old patterns to deal with an emotion they cannot cope with or understand. Looking beyond the obvious, I see the child creates chaos because, in a strange way, its familiarity is comfortable.

As our foster children grow closer to God, they will have a future and a hope in heavenly places. Their inner beauty will unfold over time, and they will become more Christlike.

Help them to look with God's perspective and realize His desire for them to become amazing. Though one style may be "in" and the other not as popular, the question of straight hair or curly becomes unimportant when we know we are made in God's image.

> *God, help us to see through Your eyes. You have made us distinct with purpose for Your glory. You treasure us, holding us close because of Your great love. Even when we stumble or do not complete work perfectly for You, it does not matter. You gave us salvation, and we are eternally grateful. We gladly give you, our lives. Amen.*

Fostering the Heart Action

Talk to the foster child about their strengths and weaknesses. Share the spiritual gifts God has given us. Ask them what they can see themselves becoming in the future and talk about reaching goals.

Going Deeper in Scripture: 2 Corinthians 3:18; Ephesians 4:24;
Colossians 3:1-4

Your Thoughts

_____

_____

_____

_____

_____

_____

_____

_____

_____

_____

_____

_____

_____

_____

_____

_____

_____

_____

_____

_____

_____

_____

49
Listen with Love

"My dear brothers and sisters, take note of this: Everyone should be quick to listen, slow to speak and slow to become angry, because human anger does not produce the righteousness that God desires."

-James 1:19-20

We received a call looking for homes for two kids. We already had several foster children, but when no one came forward to provide a placement, we asked if they could stay with us. The immediate response from the case worker was, "let me check and see if they are sexualized." The word rebounded through my mind, and I envisioned a visible X stamped on a child's head. Marked for life because they were sexually abused. But the truth is that with a lot of help and healing, even generational problems can be stopped.

An abused child is exposed to sexual stimulation before they are ready to understand or deal with the feelings attached to it. Foster parents help them through the confusion. Counselors are not with them daily; we are. As sexualized behaviors arise, we need to address them. These children are trained to believe this experience is natural. We know it is not, but for them, it can lead to difficulty differentiating between traits of positive healthy love, and dysfunction.

Some signs of sexual abuse are trying to be naked around other people, grinding, or masturbating openly, unsuitable play, inappropriate interest in sex, or being overly touchy towards others. Children who exhibit these behaviors can be of any age or gender. It is important to distinguish between expected, age-appropriate sexual awareness, and out of place behavior. If you have an uncomfortable feeling, investigate it. Talk to professionals about different options to handle the situation and ask God for discernment and wisdom to intervene on behalf of your child. Consider their unique personality, experiences, and age when deciding your next step.

When the child confides in you, the stories are hard to hear. Be prepared for your own reaction. Allow the child to speak uninterrupted and keep your emotions under control. Do not cry or become visibly mad. If you need a break, make up an excuse, go into the next room, then return when you are in control of your emotions and able to finish the conversation. Although anger is normal, keep it to yourself. The perpetrator can be someone the child knows and/or loves. A foster parent's anger only confuses them more.

When the child finishes speaking, breathe deeply and pray before you respond. It is okay to let the child know what was done to them was wrong. Assure them the abuse is not a reflection of who they are, and they are safe. When you offer advice, make sure it is age-appropriate and about subjects you are well informed. If you do not feel capable, get guidance from their counselor and/or case worker.

Go over boundaries. Your foster child will want to speak out at different points in their healing, but their friends are not at the same developmental level and cannot give them good advice. Helping your foster children to understand this serves two purposes: it protects the innocence of others, and it keeps the foster child safe from gossip. Children can be cruel to each other. Instead, give them a list of trustworthy people to whom they can express their feelings.

Our anger over our foster children's histories, even when righteous, can hold us in bondage. Putting it aside allows us to listen to and minister well to the children in our care.

> *Father, grant us wisdom to know how best to help these children.*
> *Let our vision of them be untainted by what we hear. Give us the*
> *strength to not treat them as broken, but instead to supply tools to*
> *lead an amazing life. We recognize we cannot deal with abuse*

and neglect without You, so please walk step-by-step with us.
Amen.

Fostering the Heart Action

Be intentional in the care given to your foster child. Provide opportunities to express their feelings and questions openly and safely. Check into different forms of counseling such as play therapy, horse therapy, or art expression through visual art, performance, or music.

Going Deeper in Scripture: John 8:7-11; Matthew 7:1-5; Proverbs 18:19; 1 Peter 3:8-9

Your Thoughts

_____

_____

_____

_____

_____

_____

_____

_____

_____

_____

_____

_____

_____

_____

50
Looking Past the Present

"There is a way that appears to be right,
but in the end it leads to death"

-Proverbs 14:12

She pulled up in front of the school looking for her foster child. Twenty-five minutes after searching, the missing kid threw their iPad onto the car seat and slammed the door.

They had changed into a friend's shirt, one that was not appropriate for the upcoming dance. She asked them to change their shirt when they got home. Unexpectedly, the child started yelling, "I won't be able to go..." she drove home to the sound of crying.

Entering the house, the screaming started again as doors were slammed and items from their room began to pepper the walls.

Self-sabotaging is equivalent to self-preservation for some foster children who struggle with social situations. A new and exciting event can set up the possibility of failure in their minds. Friendships are hard for any child to navigate, but for a kid who has insecurities due to past abuse, they are even harder. For this foster child, it was easier on them for their foster parent to forbid them to go, than to have to face the school dance.

The Israelites faced many hard situations leaving Egypt. They began to complain against Moses in Exodus 17:3, "Why did you bring us up out of Egypt to make us and our children and livestock die of thirst?" It appeared like Moses led them into the wrong decision. The immediate need for water overrode remembering the abuse, slavery, and death they had come from. The Israelites unknown future brought fear. Everyone has uncertainties. We will often choose to stay in our present poor circumstances because we cannot envision anything better.

Looking past the immediate reaction of your foster child is important. When their behavior is not understandable, there is a reason. Step back and look beyond appearances to seek the truth. For example, the child has been excited to visit a friend for days, but when the play time comes, their behavior becomes out of control. In exasperation, you want to refuse the activity. In reality, the child needs reassurance. Sometimes, simply giving them a hug and asking an insightful question will lead to a positive change and a growth moment.

Many times, foster children do not even understand their own reactions to circumstances. They are just becoming familiar with emotions, and the safety needed to express them. God does not want us to sabotage our own success out of fear, misunderstanding, or unworthiness. He uses all situations to increase our strength and dependence on Him.

Teaching our foster children how to embrace new experiences takes work. Every opportunity will be handled differently. After abundant assurance and affirmation, reward them with praise when they step out. Openly talk after the event, so they can see the good and learn to handle the bad. Speak gently; do not directly point out self-sabotaging behavior, but rather show them simple changes which could have smoothed things over. We cannot promise our foster children an easy life. They have big obstacles in their paths which they will have to conquer. But we can be there with a steadying hand to help them to steer away from death and do right.

> *Father, we pray for patience when confronted with an obstinate foster child. Help us to seek wisdom instead of acting in ignorance. If we are confronted with a behavior that makes no sense, help us to back off until we can come to the root of the problem. Secure our actions with Your great love. Thank You for giving us this opportunity. In the name of Jesus, amen.*

Fostering the Heart Action

The next time your foster child acts poorly when preparing for a fun activity, try circumventing their actions with an unanticipated reaction. Getting them off center may help you to open the door to real communication and transformation.

Going Deeper in Scripture: Proverbs 11:24-25; Romans 15:1-2; John 16:33

Your Thoughts

_____
_____
_____
_____
_____
_____
_____
_____
_____
_____
_____
_____
_____
_____
_____
_____
_____
_____

51
The Heart of the Broken

Cast all your anxiety on him because he cares for you.

-1 Peter 5:7

Flowers sprinkled throughout the long grass. The sun's warmth radiated against her face. Sparks reflected off the distant lake. The woman strolled through the nature which abounded around her, but unlike the peaceful setting her thoughts were of the small child back home. Her six-year-old foster daughter was on suicide watch.

This subject is hard. Our hearts break even to think a small child could even entertain the idea. How had she first heard about it? Someone that age should be playing with dolls, smiling at bubbles, and swinging on the playground.

The CDC reports suicide is the second leading cause of death for kids 10-24. The rate of suicide attempts and death is higher in foster children. Unfortunately, a lot of the signs for suicide coincide with those of kids who are in foster care.

1. Hopelessness about the future.
2. Displaying overwhelming emotional distress.
3. Changes in sleep, anger, or withdrawing from others.
4. Talking about suicide.

A police office at the local middle school stated one of the differences from his childhood to now is the widespread practice for kids to talk about suicide. He continued suicide cannot even be a thought of possibility. Our minds should never go there. He encouraged middle schoolers to talk to a trusted adult like the school counselor or foster parents.

As foster parents, we cannot change the circumstances which brought the children to us. We can help to instill a sense of belonging through family. Encourage outside activities like sports, art, robotics clubs, girl or boy scouts, and church youth groups.

Instructing the kids about Jesus Christ and His love for us. Let them know they are never alone, not only because you are there, but He is. 1 John 4:19 tells us we love Him because He first loved us.

Our past does not define us, God sent His son Jesus to teach us we are forgiven when we except him and He accepts us as we are because of His great love. This may be difficult for them to understand coming from homes of trauma and conditioned love responses. Keep reassuring them and show them through your actions what that looks like.

Tell them you love them and give hugs when appropriate. There will be kids who stiffen up in your embrace—do not take it personal. Build trust, stay consistent over time, and express unconditional love. Jesus is our example so when you do not know how to handle a situation read your Bible.

If you have an immediate threat of suicide, reach out to the professionals. You do not have to handle this alone.

> *Father we cannot heal all these precious child's wounds, so we ask You to. Help us to know how to show love, safety, and security. We pray for protection over their minds from uncertainty and fears. Lay Your arms around them providing peace and joy. Protect foster parents from the hurt which children may unintentionally inflict as they process their feelings. We need You to show us when they are in trouble then lead us in how to help. Amen*

Fostering the Heart Action

Together with your foster child, spend five minutes today talking about outlets to reduce their stress i.e., Stretching, breathing, relaxation techniques, writing, drawing, playing outdoors, or screaming into a pillow. When they get agitated or depressed remind them to use the coping skill they picked out for that situation. Be positive and praise them when they succeed. Be patient.

Going deeper in scripture: Isaiah 41:9-10, Psalm 22:24, John 16:21-23

Your Thoughts

_____
_____
_____
_____
_____
_____
_____
_____
_____
_____
_____
_____
_____
_____
_____
_____
_____
_____

52
The Decision

"Trust in the LORD with all your heart
and lean not on your own understanding;
in all your ways submit to him,
and he will make your paths straight."

-Proverbs 3:5-6

The family meeting continued. The team was split on how to proceed. In our state, the law requires that no child under age five who is removed from their home will remain away from their family beyond the one-year mark or be placed in adoption.

In the case of our foster children, a year passed. The parent was making only a minimal effort, but the courts felt the parent deserved a six-month extension of the case. Some team members disagreed. Believing the children should have the stability of a decision, so they could start *living* instead of always being pulled in different directions, waiting.

Another full year came and went. At this point, my husband and I were forty-nine and fifty-four. It was time to focus on preparation for retirement. Our adult children had reached the age to soon give us grandchildren.

The day we received the call from human services, every fiber of my being rebelled. We had not believed this question would ever come—we'd been told this would be an open and shut case. Yet here I was, on the phone with the caseworker, who was asking whether we were willing to become the children's permanent guardians.

But we had plans. We had served our time as parents. We wanted to explore parts of the world where we could never afford to go before, not start over with Disney vacations, waiting in lines for kiddie rides, children's clothes, abiding by a school schedule, and college decisions.

We loved the children, but we had never planned on raising another generation. We were faced with a hard choice. Research shows the more houses a foster kid goes through, the less likely they are to thrive. They become more vulnerable, which makes them targets for predators.

The kids had made great progress in their healing. We could not add to their feeling of being abandoned and unloved. God had called us to take in these children to begin with.

The decision was made, we became their permanent guardians.

Foster parents are repeatedly asked to do the right thing even when it is hard instead of taking the simple route. It is not something any of us sign up for, but it is part of it. We lean into God, praying He will provide us with strength, patience, loving hearts, finances, and clarity to know what is best. Our relationship with Him increases as we follow His Word. The Bible is the foundation on which we base our lives.

I do not know why God chose us to parent foster children. There are many days I would like to escape. But it is not mine to understand. I trust the Lord knows what He is doing, and His plan is perfect. I recognize that as we submit to His lead, He will bring out the best in this situation. Our culture generally teaches us to look out for ourselves, but if we all focus solely on personal need, who will look out for those who cannot take care of themselves? Children, hurting people, mentally challenged, and the elderly need Christians to model Christ's love to them.

Father, give us the ability to love beyond ourselves and our selfish desires. Meld our lives together into one family as we serve Your purpose and love the children You have given us. Provide for our needs. We do not profess to be martyrs but humble ourselves before You, because without Your grace and mercy overseeing our lives, we are nothing. Amen.

Fostering the Heart Action

What are the desires of your heart? Balance them with the true needs of your foster children. Look for ways to incorporate your wishes with the daily life of being a foster parent. You are not called to give up everything. For example, if you enjoy dinner theater, find one with a family theme and go for lunch. Or make it a special night and get a babysitter. You may have to go less often but avoid letting resentment build up by not eliminating the things you love.

Going Deeper in Scripture: James 4:17; 1 Peter 3:14; Galatians 5:19-23

Your Thoughts

_____

_____

_____

_____

_____

_____

_____

_____

_____

_____

_____

Jesus Loves You

53

God Prevails

"I am weary, God,
but I can prevail."

-Proverbs 30:1

Fostering children can be challenging. Some days feel never-ending. No matter what you do, the child still doesn't trust you, is not honest with you, or does not believe you can love them. There are many reasons for this, and none have to do with you. Foster parents receive the brunt of the behaviors the child cannot show anyone else. The kids get frustrated because they have little say in decisions made for them. Their lives and emotions are swung on a pendulum of people peering into, but not *living*, their lives. The courts, child protective services, the counselors, their biological parents, and their foster parents are all a part of the pieces put together to hopefully come up with the best solution to the current circumstances.

The child's past affects every aspect of their life. They have misconceptions of how to express love, interact with people, and what a healthy life is. Priorities are confused; expectations of who they should be and how to deal with their emotions are skewed.

Foster parents take on all these burdens. In loving these kids, we try to be good examples and integrate their worlds with ours. Our job is huge and many days we can be left discouraged, hurt, and wondering if we will ever make a difference.

The Bible tells us God is our strength. You are not expected to do this alone, even though the task can feel lonely. Cry out to God. He will pick up our heavy loads and carry us through, making our burdens light. When we want to give up, we need to pray, read the Bible, and seek out others who can encourage.

Foster parents can prevail. We are strong, otherwise we would not have volunteered to be in this position. As seed planters, God empowers us, but ultimately, He is the only one who can heal these children. God uses us to help lead foster children to a more abundant life. He takes the seeds we plant, waters them with other people's spiritual gifts. Over the years, He plows the fields with new experiences. All these things combine to form new beings out of our foster children.

Sometimes foster parents can feel they have let the kids down or have not done enough to help. All we can do is our best. When you feel like you've failed, remember God says each day is new in Him. If you need to ask forgiveness, then do it. Should you need more knowledge on how to handle something, learn it. On days when you're tired and need a break, ask for it.

You do not expect foster children to be perfect, do you? Then let go of the burden you place on yourself. God sees us as a work in progress. We are only learning to be more like Him; *we are not Him.*

When you're disappointed in yourself, remember there was only one perfect person, and His name was Jesus. The rest of us are paint strokes on a canvas adding detail. The work is never complete. Call out to the Heavenly Father when you are weary, He will listen, comfort, and provide for you. If you feel like no one understands you, He does. He sees your heart, your inmost being, your intimate thoughts. He loves you when you make mistakes or masterpieces. God will take your weariness from you today, tomorrow, and through eternity.

God loves your foster child even more than you do. He will be there when you are not. God's plan is greater than what takes place today.

Father, pardon us when we make a mistake. When we cannot let go and we allow weariness to enter our souls, release us from the bondage of our self-criticism. Help us to use all You are teaching

us to become more like You. Help us to prevail so that we may
love these children with Your agape love. Amen.

Fostering the Heart Action

When weariness overwhelms you, take a break. Spend time in silence, opening your mind to hear what God wants for you. Forgive yourself for any perceived mistake. God has. There is nothing He cannot redeem. Do not give the enemy power to keep you from moving forward.

Going Deeper in Scripture: Matthew 11:28; Galatians 6:9; Isaiah 40:31

Your Thoughts

_____

_____

_____

_____

_____

_____

_____

_____

_____

_____

_____

_____

_____

54

Today Changes Tomorrow

"Yet this I call to mind. and therefore I have hope: Because of the LORD's great love we are not consumed, for his compassions never fail. They are new every morning; great is your faithfulness."
-Lamentations 3:21-23

It was one of those moments when you either hit bottom or experience an awakening. Whichever it was for me, it came that day. I realized there was no going back to the "easy, good days." My life had become complicated, and I had to acknowledge it as my new normal existence.

I wanted to figure out how to blend my vision for myself and my life, with my current reality. Trusting God's plan for my future felt like a greater task than I could handle. I began to examine where I currently was in life contrasted to what life could become.

Overwhelmed thoughts ran rampant, fighting for dominance. Should I start with losing weight, eating healthy, exercising, writing, being a more attentive wife, or being the best foster mom I could be to help heal precious children? Added to this was my derogatory self-talk of *fat, old, unworthy, harsh,* and *impatient.* How could I possibly think I could raise children? I was looking at a lot of hard personal work.

It helps combat the lies of the enemy when we remember that the God of the universe sees you and me as His children, ones He loves, cares for, understands, and accepts just as we are. The evil one wants failure, to cause self-hate and make life a burden instead of a blessing, so we cannot achieve what God intends.

I recognized what I had become happened over time. I could not undo the things I didn't like instantly. Realizing actions today will change my tomorrow, I began to focus on just one day. This one day became important, with all the promise of a future yet to tell.

The little details of a day influence those around us, too. A kind word of encouragement can inspire someone. Opposite to this, hate-filled accusations can bring destruction. We make conscious decisions about how we change our world. This was brought home to me when I met a friend along a riverbank. She was staring off into the distance, but I interrupted her thoughts. It was a five-minute conversation that could have taken place anywhere and cost me nothing. A few days later she came to me, expressing her gratitude. God gave me the exact words she needed to hear. This ended up influencing a decision that was life-changing for her.

We cannot do anything without God. He gives us vision, strength, and wisdom, which allow us to become all He intends. If this were not true, you wouldn't be reading this now. It is a sad fact that I am a terrible communicator, yet God has chosen to give me desire to write His words. We are all blessed with gifts that He wants us to use to enrich the world around us. Frighteningly though, the tormentor of our soul also knows our weaknesses and will use all means to try to stop what God intends for good. Be aware, focus on today, and tomorrow God will bring you to heavenly places.

> *Father, I pray we will make slight changes today, which flow into our futures, so we will become the people we are meant to be. Help us to let go of past hurts and mistakes, even if they were yesterday, forgiving ourselves and those around us. We ask for Your vision and strength to make a step now toward the future. Amen*

Fostering the Heart Action

Take a moment to envision something you would like for your future. Is it a habit you need to break, a ministry you would like to have, or a relationship which needs repair? Ask God to lead you. Start today with one step toward your desire.

Going Deeper in Scripture: 2 Corinthians 4:16-18; Deuteronomy 31:6; 1 John 3:2

Your Thoughts

_____

_____

_____

_____

_____

_____

_____

_____

_____

_____

_____

_____

_____

_____

_____

_____

_____

_____

_____

_____

55
Multitude of Voices

"Then I heard what sounded like a great multitude, like the roar
of rushing waters and like loud peals of thunder, shouting:
"Hallelujah! For our Lord God Almighty reigns."
-Revelation 19:6

Amidst the chaos of raising foster children, we can overlook the achievements. Changes can be minor overtime, so we do not recognize them. It takes a small event to remember where the child started from when they came into our homes.

Our foster child tripped over a rut in the road and tore up their knees on the rock and dirt. After a trip to the emergency room, I remarked offhandedly how this child would always find their way home. Hallelujah—how God has worked in this child's life. Where once, they got lost while playing in a small, roped off toy area, they now could find our home from a distance while in pain and hurt. How they had grown!

When we see an achievement, our human nature can want to grab on to it as our own doing, but when we are honest, there is no way we can produce the amazing changes that occur in these children apart from God. He gives us the patience, kindness, insight, direction, and continual love to give foster kids.

I join the angels in rejoicing in the Lord God Almighty who reigns. He brought the initial awareness that allowed these children to be removed from the bondage of abuse, neglect, or hardship. God prepared us, walks with us, and gives us the desire to be great foster parents. If all the pieces had not fit together in one precise way, these children would not be healing, and maturing into healthy adults. On our own we stumble, but with Him we are strong.

This weekend when you take your foster child to church you will be giving them the greatest treasure. If you do not have a home church, ask friends for referrals. It is important to start learning about God for yourself and your foster children. You will be with the kids for a brief time, but God will be with them forever. If you plant seeds of faith now, it will give the child a rock to stand on when things get rough in the future. Life always has ups and downs and teaching them about God and the Bible gives them tools to cope with good and bad times.

As our foster children become compassionate, empathetic, educated, stronger, vital, and find their identity in Christ and not in their past, we can all join in praising the Lord. Psalm 100:1-3 says, "Shout for joy to the LORD, all the earth. Worship the LORD with gladness; come before him with joyful songs. Know that the LORD is God. It is he who made us, and we are his; we are his people, the sheep of his pasture." God knew us in the womb of our mothers, He knows what we will do every day of our life, and yet He still loves us.

There are many milestones as your foster children develop. We are blessed to be a part of this important work. Rejoicing with them in their triumphs is a kindness God gives us as we work in partnership with Him.

Abba Father, thank You for bringing these children out of broken homes and providing caseworkers, CASA members, guardians ad litem, and foster families with the desire to save children's lives and to fight for them because they count. All Your children are valuable and important. We praise You for loving us so much You gave us Your Son to show us what we are called to be. Without Your splendor we would be nothing. We join our voices to the Heavenly hosts praising You for your magnificence. Amen.

Fostering the Heart Action

Take the next ten minutes to praise God for the little things He has done in your and your foster child's lives.

Going Deeper in Scripture: Psalm 103:1-5; Colossians 3:16; Zephaniah 3:17

Your Thoughts

_____

_____

_____

_____

_____

_____

_____

_____

_____

_____

_____

_____

_____

_____

_____

_____

_____

_____

56
When I Rise

*"I in them and you in me—so that they may be brought to
complete unity. Then the world will know that you sent me and
have loved them even as you have loved me."*

-John 17:23

The early morning hours, when the sky is just starting to
lighten, is the timeframe when I hear God with consistent clarity. For
me it is the quiet of our home, before children awaken, the time when
even the dog still sleeps. In the stillness, God talks to me in His infinite
holiness. He fills my soul with His words. He rejoices in a new day with
me. It is a time when I am in unity with Jesus, The Father, and the
Holy Spirit. Because I am refreshed, and I am ready to listen.

"This is what the LORD says, he who made the earth, the
LORD who formed it and established it—the LORD is his name: 'Call
to me and I will answer you and tell you great and unsearchable things
you do not know'" (Jeremiah 33:2-3).

Is it not amazing that the God who created the universe loves
you? That He considers your calls to Him significant enough to answer
personally? He does not delegate to someone else. He allows us to talk
directly to Him in prayer, and He answers. Through the intimacy of
your personal conversation with Himself, He shows you things you
would never have known.

We invite God into our lives through prayer, opening our
minds and hearts for His instruction. But we can shut Him out too.
What happens when you do not like what He tells you? "Love your
neighbor as yourself" (Mark 12:31) can be an obstacle when you or

your foster child has been hurt by them. Or when God asks us to be patient (Colossians 3:12) instead of getting angry. If we ask to hear from Him, then we must be ready to accept the instruction and put our trust in the truth that He knows and sees everything. He can put the pieces together when they make no sense to us. He does this to perfect us. 2 Corinthians 4:16-18 tells us not to lose heart. What trouble we have is outweighed by what we are achieving. God calls us to not focus on what we see, but on what is unseen, because it is eternal. There is hope in that.

The best news is we are not doing it all alone, but in unity with God. Because He loves us, He will not leave us to face foster parenting alone. As Christians, He wants us to be unified as a witness to what He can accomplish through us. Jesus says when we stay in line with Him, we can do amazing work.

When we try to accomplish the healing of our foster children by ourselves, we become tired, disappointed, and unforgiving. We can want to give up. Allow God to restore you.

The time of day you're most drawn to sit with Him may be like mine, at the first pinking of the sky when dew or frost still lay on the ground. Or it could be a moment like a hike through the mountains on a sunny afternoon when warmth touches your skin. It could even be the evening when the busyness of the day has settled, and you find rest in the comfort of a soft, cozy blanket, and a cup of tea is when you align your heart with Jesus. Whenever it is, make a conscious effort to spend time with God every day. He will speak to you, teach you, nurture you, and refill you with His holy presence; just ask.

> *My Heavenly Father, you are so precious to our sight. We live to know You more. Today, we pray for a quiet moment, wrapped in Your love, to feel Your holy presence where we can learn more of Your character. Help us to see Your desires and follow through on what we've seen. Strengthen our abilities to foster a child. We recognize we cannot fix this situation on our own and we invite You to lead the way. Amen.*

Fostering the Heart Action

Take a minute and consider your current schedule. What time of day is most restful to you? Is there a special place you feel more at ease? Then intentionally add time for reflection, restoration, and prayer to each day. If there is a day which allows you several hours, wonderful plan on utilizing it. But even when you can only carve out fifteen minutes, use it for a visit with the Father, the Son, and the Holy Ghost.

Going Deeper in Scripture: John 1:1-5; John 15:4-5; 2 Corinthians 13:14

Your Thoughts

_____

_____

_____

_____

_____

_____

_____

_____

_____

_____

_____

_____

_____

_____

_____

57

Perpetuating Peace

"Do not let any unwholesome talk come out of your mouths, but only what is helpful for building others up according to their needs, that it may benefit those who listen. And do not grieve the Holy Spirit of God, with whom you were sealed for the day of redemption. Get rid of all bitterness, rage and anger, brawling and slander, along with every form of malice. Be kind and compassionate to one another, forgiving each other, just as in Christ God forgave you. Follow God's example, therefore, as dearly loved children and walk in the way of love, just as Christ loved us and gave himself up for us as a fragrant offering and sacrifice to God."

-Ephesians 4:29-5:2

Life is noisy. It is full of activity, conflicting viewpoints, and too many electronic devices. I find myself striving for peace. I prepared for my mission trip to Guatemala looking forward to the simplicity of less distraction. No appointments, nightly homework, childish arguments between kids, or running from place to place to pick up my foster children.

Towards the end of the trip, I found myself packed into a small bus jammed with people. Conversations flowed around me in different languages overlapping each other. Pressed in between my foster child on one side and a woman who spoke only Spanish on the other, and the aisleway blocked with people, escape was impossible. It was in that confusing jumbled moment that God spoke to me. "This, my child, is peace. When my people from different walks in life join with one voice, heart, and actions for my single purpose."

My mistake is thinking I must be alone and surrounded by quiet to hear God's voice, but that is not true. We only need to be open to it. Our Father is almighty, powerful. He reigns over all when we open our hearts to Him. Everyone is unique, God has given each person different skills, abilities, desires, likes and interests. He uses these to help us connect with other people and with our foster children.

When we accept Christ as our Savior, God gives us additional spiritual gifts like prophecy, serving, teaching, encouraging, giving, leading, or showing mercy (Romans 12:6). Our gift is of no use if we hold onto it for ourselves, but when we give it freely in conjunction with other followers of Christ, we can accomplish amazing miracles from God. During our Guatemala mission trip, our group built five houses with stoves and furniture, led Bible school for adults/children, and provided useful everyday items. We ministered to displaced volcano victims who had lost homes, family members, and had scars emotionally and physically. God accomplished a lot through us.

As foster parents, when we work with the team overseeing the child/children's care, it can become noisy with conflicting viewpoints and augmentative behavior. When we stop and listen to one another, each team member contributes something different. Working together under the authority of Christ, we achieve His purpose. Not all team members are believers. As Christians we choose to allow our actions to be a testimony to those around us. Go to prayer when everything gets convoluted and ask God to intervene.

Peace is not the absence of noise. According to the Merriam-Webster dictionary[3], peace is freedom from disquieting or oppressive thoughts or emotions, and harmony in personal relations. The more we become like Christ, our fragrance becomes a sweeter offering to God.

---

[3] Merriam-Webster, s.v. "peace (n)," accessed March 25, 2019, http://www.merriam-webster.com/dictionary/peace

Father, thank You for giving us the Bible filled with knowledge to help us live in peace. Where there is strife in our hearts, take it from us, renewing us in Your Spirit so we may be living examples of who You are. Give us eyes to see what You want us to accomplish and the drive to do it. Let us align our lives to Your will so we may live in peace. Amen.

Fostering the Heart Action

Read the Ephesians scripture once again. Pick out one area from that passage that you need to change so peace may increase in your home, then work on implementing new strategies, or look at it from a different viewpoint.

Going Deeper in Scripture: Colossians 3:15; James 3:18; John 14:27

Your Thoughts

_____

_____

_____

_____

_____

_____

_____

_____

_____

_____

_____

58
Overcoming Uncertainty

"God is our refuge and strength,
an ever-present help in trouble.
Therefore we will not fear, though the earth give way
and the mountains fall into the heart of the sea,"

-Psalm 46:1-2

Uncertainty surrounded me, the future unknown. Exhaustion due to sleep loss did not help my state of mind either.

Even when things are going well, there are moments when we doubt. But in unrest, failure, or pain, doubt can pile on in mountainous heaps. It is in those times we should turn to God. Unfortunately, it typically seems easier to avoid facing these situations through escape into entertainment, alcohol, work, or activity. We all have a vice we lean into. Mine is ignoring it by going into survival mode and wishing the circumstances would resolve themselves instead of facing them. This does not work very well and causes stress beyond measure.

We do not know what the future holds, only this spot in time. We can get stuck in past failure or history when we cling to it, whether it be in a desire to hold onto something you loved that is now gone, or a hurt too awful to face. God wants you to overcome and mature into the person He has created you to be. That's right, God has a vested interest in you. He wants you to succeed, He hears your cries, and He loves you even when you immerse yourself in bad choices.

God gave us relationship with Him and others to encourage us. A friend can speak a word which brings you back to the hope we have in Christ. He provided some with the gift of music so songs can minister to our hearts on the radio. Preachers teach us what it means to know more of God and how to apply Bible verses in daily life. None of us can do it by ourselves. We need community.

Stress, worry, or hardship can make you want to withdraw to lick your wounds. Those are the days when you do not want to see a single soul. Conversation with other people feels trite, tiring, or hypocritical. When you go to church or visit friends, you put on a happy "mask," so no one knows what is going on. We, Christians, believe because we follow Christ, we are supposed to be able to handle anything, right? A well-meaning friend might say, "God does not give you more than you can handle." But He does. It is a tool He uses to develop us and make us more dependent on Him. It is at these moments we must set aside our pride and reach out to others. Recognizing you cannot hold everything inside is a true step toward healing and overcoming obstacles.

Everyone has down days; it is normal. God does not expect us to be perfect, just honest. Psalm 55:2 tells us, "Cast your cares on the LORD and he will sustain you; he will never let the righteous be shaken." He is here to carry your burdens, listen to your innermost thoughts, and pull you through the difficulties. God is not fear; He is hope. "For the Spirit God gave us does not make us timid, but gives us power, love, and self-discipline" (2 Timothy 1:7). He never leaves us.

Abba Father, we need You. Life is hard sometimes and the overwhelming trials can make us doubtful. The enemy of our soul whispers hateful things in our ears. Block the untruth and fill us with Your light and presence. When we become desperate, help us to lean on You and not worldly vices which distract and destroy. You are our refuge, hope, and greatest supporter. May the love You provide overcome all obstacles. Amen.

Fostering the Heart Action

Call a godly friend, offer up your inner thoughts, and let God minister to you through that person. Keep your ears open for the whispers of God all around you. If you are the friend being reached out to, listen. Do not advice unless God gives you a specific word. Your presence and caring are all your friend needs.

Going Deeper in Scripture: Matthew 11:28; Hebrews 4:16; John 14:27

Your Thoughts

_____

_____

_____

_____

_____

_____

_____

_____

_____

_____

_____

_____

_____

_____

_____

_____

_____

_____

_____

_____

59
Do Not Doubt

"Lord, if it's you,' Peter replied, 'tell me to come to you on the water.' 'Come,' he said. Then Peter got down out of the boat, walked on the water and came toward Jesus. But when he saw the wind, he was afraid and, beginning to sink, cried out, 'Lord, save me!' Immediately Jesus reached out his hand and caught him. 'You of little faith,' he said, 'why did you doubt?'"

-Matthew 14:28-31

There are people who listen to a teacher once and know the answers to the problem immediately. I am not one of those people. In elementary school, I was placed in special reading classes. They thought I could not comprehend, but the problem was soon diagnosed. I was an incredibly slow reader. Unfortunately, the solution to my problem came too late; my self-doubt had already been established. I would not raise my hand in class. I lost faith in myself to know the correct answer. Where once I would participate enthusiastically, I hesitated instead, afraid of opening myself up to ridicule.

During college I discovered that for me to learn, I needed to read something, write it in my own words, then study from my writing. Finding this out allowed me to finish my college years with A's. But it all still sticks with me: the stigma and doubt of special classes, the laughter of other children at my mispronunciations, and all those C's during my twelve years of primary school and my first year of college.

When my foster child corrects my pronunciation, the hurt came rolling back. I knew I could let the pain stop me from fostering this child, or I could see myself through God's eyes and use it to parent better the next time my foster child makes a mistake.

Planting doubts about your ability is a tool used by the enemy. He says we have limitations. God says we can do anything with Him. When God gave Jeremiah the position of prophet to Israel, Jeremiah answered him saying, "*Alas, Sovereign Lord, "I said, "I do not know how to speak; I am too young*" (Jeremiah 1:6). God replied that He would give Jeremiah words to speak. Jeremiah's faith in God gave him the ability to be a prophet for 41 years and to serve five different kings. Where the enemy wanted to use Jeremiah's insecurities to stop him, God gave him assurance in his abilities.

As a foster parent, you will hit dark moments. When you think, *God, I cannot help this child*, or, *I don't have the stamina to keep this child any longer,* remember *you* do not, but God does. Invite God into the situation. Ask Him to guide you in finetuning your skills. Perhaps you need further knowledge, then take an additional class. Think back on your lifetime—is there a situation that was similar? How did God get you through? When using the talents God has given you, do not let your inner self-talk stop you. If God has given you a nudge to foster a child, teach, encourage, or nurture, do it.

God has laid out an opportunity before you, be confident and do not doubt. Keep faith He has chosen you for a purpose and given you the resources to accomplish His work. When the wind comes up and the waves begin to crash, Jesus will catch your hand and pull you to safety.

> *Father, we pray You will show us our path. Give us the tools to accomplish the tasks we are asked to do and the courage to follow through with Your work. When doubts fill our mind, remove them, and replace them with faith in You to accomplish all things. Let us come to know You through the process in a more intimate way. Amen.*

Fostering the Heart Action

When you have doubts, think over the past and recognize where they might have come from, then lay them before the Lord and ask Him to take the burden. Realize it is okay to be reliant on God to provide for the situation. You are not alone. If the doubt was someone else's and they came to you to ask about it, would you encourage them differently than you do yourself? Change your perspective from *impossible* to *possible with God.*

Going Deeper in Scripture: Proverbs 3:5-8; Matthew 21:21; Genesis 3:1

Your Thoughts

_____

_____

_____

_____

_____

_____

_____

_____

_____

_____

_____

_____

_____

_____

60
A Recessive Gene

"You, God, are my God,
earnestly I seek you; I thirst for you,
my whole being longs for you,
in a dry and parched land
where there is no water."

-Psalm 63:1

As a young adult, I yearned for something to fill a need within me I did not understand. I visited 14 countries, went to two different universities, and had a couple of long-term relationships. After every new experience, I would be satisfied for a short while, but it would not take long before I became dissatisfied and began the search again. When I gave birth to my daughter a piece of the void was filled with life. I was able to express my love, and frankly I was too busy to keep looking, but even my baby could not fill the hole.

There are many times in our lives when we look to worldly things to fulfill our desires, only to end up in a dry and parched land. It can take the form of an exciting relationship, a better job, a new cell phone, or escaping through alcohol, porn, or going to a show. Anything we become obsessive toward only provides temporary relief. It does not make us complete. A perfect child initially gives us a sense of awe at the unexplainable ability to create life, but eventually we forget as we get busy taking care of the child.

My baby daughter and I once stood in line at the grocery store. A man behind us commented on how beautiful my baby was and asked if she were mine. I was often asked this question because of the striking difference in our coloring. My baby had light blond hair and big blue eyes, whereas I had dark brown hair and hazel eyes. When I answered yes, he responded, "Oh, you must have a recessive gene."

A recessive gene is not apparent on the surface but is within you. In order to have a child with blue eyes, both parents must give the blue-eyed gene to the child.

We all have a recessive gene. It is the thirst of our soul which yearns for something unexplainable. God placed the desire in our hearts for a relationship with him.

In Genesis, Adam and Eve started in perfect harmony with God. They lived side by side and had no cares. When their sin entered, God kicked them out of the refuge He created and made them work to survive. They did not know they were going to miss the relationship with God until it was too late. Romans 3:23 states, "for all have sinned and fall short of the glory of God."

When we do something wrong, we know it. We can tell ourselves it is okay because we are not hurting anyone else, but that is a fabrication of our minds to justify our behavior. When we recognize this, we turn, searching for answers for why we feel so hollow. "And all are justified freely by his grace through the redemption that came by Christ Jesus" (Romans 3:24).

It is only by accepting Jesus as our Savior that the void is filled. He gives us the Holy Spirit to reside within us, slacking our thirst, satisfying our needs, and giving us purpose. Only God can love us, even when we falter. He holds us when we cry, walks with us as we contemplate our steps, and runs next to us in our excitement.

Father, we lift our hearts, minds, and beings, praying You will calm our restless nature. Help us to stop looking in places You don't dwell—in the things that are temporary in life. Instead, let us be made whole through our relationship with You. We pray we will give up on the things in our lives which are elusive and instead reach for the God of our hearts who knows us intimately. Amen.

Fostering the Heart Action

Seek God by pursing Him intentionally. Read your Bible daily. Pray as the sun rises, sets, and every moment in between. Take quiet time and meditate on one word for personal growth, for example, joy, patience, or perseverance. Go for a walk and look for the beauty God created. Recognize the intricacies of life. God will meet you in the moment.

Going Deeper in Scripture: Psalm 63:1; John 3:16-17; Act 4:12

Your Thoughts

_____

_____

_____

_____

_____

_____

_____

_____

_____

_____

_____

_____

_____

_____

_____

When Foster
Children Leave

61
Grief

"The righteous cry out, and the Lord hears them;
He delivers them from all their troubles.
The Lord is close to the brokenhearted
and saves those who are crushed in spirit."

Psalm 34:17-18

When your heart breaks, watching the foster child pack their belongings to head back to their birth parents or another placement, it is difficult. Pushing my thoughts away, to stem the tears, I slipped into a halfhearted smile trying to be happy for them. It took weeks for my crying to end and to look at their leaving as a positive step in their healing.

Children want their biological parents. They identify with them. For those of us raised in healthy households, it can be hard to understand why they want to go back. There is a piece of them which is missing. They need love from that one person or family who should have loved them safely to begin with.

For me— my spirit was crushed.

As foster parents, we pour into these children for months or years. You cannot help but form an attachment. The desire to see their faces after school or to miss tucking them into bed. They were a part of your daily family life. Sometimes you are blessed to have an open relationship with their parent or guardians and will get to continue to see them, but other times when they leave; you are cut off. It could be distance, or social services. The parent may feel jealous over your influence on the child. The children learned to turn to you but now they must seek their parent or guardian.

It is normal to grieve even when you are happy for them that their family has healed enough to care for them. Perhaps it will comfort you to know, Romans 8:28 tells us "God works for the good of those who love him, who have been called according to his purpose. For God foreknew he also predestined to be conformed to the likeness of his Son." God used you to fulfill His great purpose of healing a foster child. As a Christian, we aim to be more like Christ. You have grown, the child has grown, and God who loves you gave you an amazing opportunity to become more like Him.

The time you spent with the child will not come back void. God will use every moment and word to speak to your foster child.

If you ask, God will be here for you now. He will wrap His arms around you when you feel alone. He will listen to your cry, wipe away your tears, and heal your brokenness. It may not feel like it at the moment, but it was all worth it. God will take your crushed spirit, mend it, and lift you up to see your new beginning.

Father, we turn our grief over to you and ask you to heal the pieces that have broken. We pray we will see the bigger picture of what you are doing. Give us hope and rebuild our strength as you lead us moving forward. We ask You to be with our foster child. Give them peace and protection. We pray over their parents or guardians and their home that you would continue the work which has started in them. Let them see your touch today in the little moments. Amen.

Fostering the Heart Action

Take a moment to be grateful. You have helped a family in an incredibly special way. When you are sad, surround yourself with family or friends. Remember you make a difference.

Going Deeper in Scripture: Psalm 73:26, Matthew 5:4, Psalm 23

Your Thoughts

62
Letting Go

"There is a time for everything,
and a season for every activity under the heavens:"

Ecclesiastes 3:1

Looking out over the Colorado mountains this morning, I wonder what it was like the moment they were created. A quick google search tells me it took more than a minute. It took the plates below the mountains scrapping against each other twice. But that was only the beginning, volcanos erupted, oceans covered them a couple times, and glaciers moved the rock and dirt. This transformation reflects our time with our foster children. There was not one step but a multitude which brought them to the point of leaving our homes.

Ecclesiastes 3:11, "...He has also set eternity in the hearts of men; yet they cannot fathom what God has done from the beginning to end." We may not be able to grasp the making of the Rocky Mountains, but God is eternal. A moment for Him is millions of years to us. He knows yesterday, today, and tomorrow. He is infinite. He knows what is ahead for you and your foster child.

After His creation, God left us to see soaring rocky peaks of snow topped mountains covered by beautiful golden aspen and evergreens perched in stony soils. In our limited imagination, we could not have created the scent of pines after rain or the majestic bugle of a bull elk standing over his herds. God had a vision and He fulfilled it.

He knows what He is doing for you and your foster child too. He took the upheaval of their lives and placed them in your care. You watched over them helping them to heal and get through the rocky hills of life. Now, He is removing the children from your home so He can continue the lifetime of work He has planned for them and you.

Our prayers will be our battle ground for them now. We will ask for protection from the enemy and join the Holy Spirit with intercessory prayer. We will reach out to our foster children, if allowed, reminding them they are important and made in God's image.

God has a new plan He has formed for you now. What that is, only He and you will discover. He may have you take on more children or it may be a time of new work. He will take the knowledge you have gained and apply it to the next adventure. Perhaps it is time to rest.

I cannot say it any better than Ecclesiastes 3:2-10, "a time to be born and a time to die,

a time to plant and a time to uproot,
a time to kill and a time to heal,
a time to tear down and a time to build,
a time to weep and a time to laugh,
a time to mourn and a time to dance,
a time to scatter stones and a time to gather them,
a time to embrace and a time to refrain from embracing,
a time to search and a time to give up,
a time to keep and a time to throw away,
a time to tear and a time to mend,
a time to be silent and a time to speak,
a time to love and a time to hate,
a time for war and a time for peace.

What do workers gain from their toil? I have seen the burden God has laid on the human race. He has made everything beautiful in its time."

Now trust God to make everything beautiful once again. Your work is complete.

Father, we thank you for loving us. We pray for your peace, understanding, guidance, and faith to step forward into the next step of your plan. We give you our lives as we begin again. Amen

Fostering the Heart Action

It is time to let go. Take a moment to thank God for all He has done and will do in you and your foster child's life. Give yourself permission to rest.

Thank you for being a foster parent.

Your Thoughts

_____

_____

_____

_____

_____

_____

_____

_____

_____

_____

_____

_____

_____

_____

_____

_____

_____

_____

_____

Closing Thoughts

Dear readers, we step into foster parenting with the hope and desire that our love will change the life of a child. What we learn is the child needs more than a warm house and healthy food. They need to be equipped to heal so they can flourish. These amazing children are strong survivors. God gave them dreams, talents, beauty, minds, and hearts which can overcome their past to a mighty future. You are their guide to a full and rich life in Christ. Some days are hope filled trials while others joy filled triumphs, but with God's grace and strength you grow in faith and fulfill your purpose.

Families need the community of Christ. When we work together to ensure the health of children, society will thrive. There are many organizations out there who work alongside foster parents. Local churches, government agencies, and national non-profit organizations provide support and information. For those of us who do not live close to any resources, we can watch webinars or read books to supplement our knowledge on the care of these precious children.

God calls us to Isaiah 1:17, "Learn to do right; seek justice. Defend the oppressed. Take up the cause of the fatherless; plead the case of the widow." We are in His hands. Thank you for opening your homes and loving the abused, neglected, or alone children of our world.

Bibliography

Center for Disease Control and Prevention, National Center for Health Statistics. National Vital Statistics System, Mortality 2018-2021 on CDC WONDER Online Database, released in 2021. Data are from the Multiple Cause of Death files, 2018-2021, as compiled from data provided by the 57 vital statistics jurisdictions through Viral Statistics Cooperative Program. Accessed at http://wonder.cdc.gov/ucd-icd10-expanded.html on Apr 9,2024

Page 6 Brown, Jennifer, 2024, *It costs Colorado $343,453 per kid who ages out of foster care according to new research.* The Colorado Sun, accessed March 2024, **https://coloradosun.com/2023/11/15/it-costs-colorado-343453-per-kid-who-ages-out-of-foster-care-according-to-new-research/**

Page 7 Stout, Jordan M Braciszewski and Rober L, 2012, *Substance Use Among Current and Former Foster You: A systematic Review,* PMC PubMed Central, accessed March 2024, **https://www.ncbi.nlm.nih.gov/pmc/articles/PMC3596821/**

About the Author

Niki Barlow is an author, blogger, speaker, and foster child advocate. Her passion for people and love of God inspires her writings. Niki is no stranger to the sting of pain, tears that flow, unexpected challenges, discouragement and adversities, but through God's grace she knows true joy. Niki and her husband Richard have been married 22 years and raised seven beautiful children.

If you have any thoughts, questions, or need a listening ear, I would love to hear from you at fosteringtheheart@gmail.com. To follow Fostering the Heart check out our website at **https://Fosteringtheheart.com.** It provides access to blogs, books, mentorship, and speaking arrangements. For additional devotions, you may follow my blog at https://nikibarlow.wordpress.com/.

www.ingramcontent.com/pod-product-compliance
Lightning Source LLC
Chambersburg PA
CBHW071425090426
42737CB00011B/1574